THE SAGE OF BETHANY

To my friend and fellow-
Minister Donald Ford.
in appreciation of your
Generous Spirit and many
acts of Christian kindness
Ralph Richardson

THE SAGE OF BETHANY

A PIONEER IN BROADCLOTH

Compiled by

Perry E. Gresham

THE BETHANY PRESS—ST. LOUIS, MO.

Library of Congress Catalog Card Number: 60-14651

Printed in the United States of America

Introduction

These essays were suggested by the late Oreon E. Scott of St. Louis, Missouri, who contemplated a $25,000 endowment for an Alexander Campbell Lectureship at Bethany College. The untimely death of Mr. Scott interrupted the series before this noble philanthropist had time to segregate the funds for the endowment. The college has continued the program with some help from the Oreon E. Scott Foundation in order that this volume in honor of Mr. Campbell might be completed.

The lecturers have been very generous with their time and attention in order that the manuscripts might be prepared for publication, since a public address does not always lend itself to the purpose of printing without some modifications. I have attempted to bring the essays together into a sort of logical sequence. The opening essay is an overview of Campbell's life, giving emphasis to his educational views which founded Bethany College where the lectures were delivered. This first chapter was presented in its original form before the Western Pennsylvania Historical Society, and printed in the *Western Pennsylvania Historical Magazine,* Volume 41, Number 1, Spring, 1958. The subsequent essays are somewhat more analytical, showing the various aspects of the life and times of Alexander Campbell. I am grateful to all who have helped in this preparation, but especially to Doctor Wilbur Haverfield Cramblet, President of the Christian Board of Publication, and former President of Bethany College, who has devoted the time and talent of his professional staff to the technical preparation of this volume.

Perry E. Gresham, Editor
Bethany College, 1959

Contents

Alexander Campbell—Schoolmaster

PERRY EPLER GRESHAM

President of Bethany College and author of
Disciplines of the High Calling

A family reunion on a dusty wagon road just east of Chestnut Ridge on October 19, 1809, seems scarcely worth remembering. Yet this reunion marks the beginning of an interesting development in American history. Alexander Campbell, then 21, was bringing his mother, two brothers, and four sisters to join his father Thomas Campbell, who preceded his family by two years in their emigration to America. Thomas Campbell was a Seceder Presbyterian preacher from Ahorey, Ireland, who had the interesting habit of starting a private school wherever he happened to live. His parentage was Scottish even though he was Irish born. His education consisted of a full undergraduate course at the University of Glasgow with the additional seminary training provided by the Seceder Church, which consisted of five terms of eight weeks each. His scholarly nature and discipline enabled him to read widely in the fields of literature and philosophy as well as theology. In two short American years he had not only managed to get himself tried for heresy but also to form an association for the promotion of religion and morality which was destined to become the largest religious body of American origin which today claims 3,500,000 adult communicants in its two major branches.

His brilliant son, Alexander, was delighted to find his father had broken with the sectarian traditions of the Seceders, since his own spiritual pilgrimage had prompted him virtually to separate himself from the church in Glasgow by refusing communion. The incidents leading up to the reunion on the road were dramatic. The family had started to America in 1808 but a shipwreck off the Hebrides sent them back to Oban and down the coast to Glasgow where Alexander rounded out his private education with a good solid year in the sciences and literature at the University of Glasgow. The voyage in 1809 was successful. Fifty-four days on the water brought them to New York on September 29 whence they journeyed by coach to Philadelphia. With Washington, Pennsylvania, as their destination they started on the deliberate journey westward by wagon.

Three days' journey from the reunion on the road brought the Campbell family to Washington, which was then a small village of some 500 inhabitants. On the way Thomas told his son of the Christian Association. He was eager for Alexander to read the proof sheets of "The Declaration and Address," a document signed by 21 men but written by Thomas Campbell, as the principles underlying the newly formed association. The party crossed the Monongahela River into Washington County by ferry at a place then called Williamsport. At their arrival in the village they settled down to a destiny that would start two academies, a college, a state, and a new communion.

Within a short space of two years the Christian Association of Washington County, Pennsylvania, had become a new and separate religious communion with its headquarters in a small country church erected on Brush Run about two miles up from Buffalo Creek; Alexander had been licensed to preach; and "The Declaration and Address" had become an important historical document with a significant destiny. The "Declaration" set forth the ambitious aims of the Association as "to restore the unity, peace, and purity of the whole Church of God." This was followed by Thomas Campbell's "Address" which outlined the principles for restoring the "unity, peace, and purity" of the church. The first words of the "Address" laid down the fundamental concept that "The Church of Christ is essentially, intentionally, and constitutionally one." Elaborating principles include the rejection of all human creeds in favor of the Scripture as the only binding articles of faith with the New Testament as the "perfect constitution" for the Church. Divisions among Christians were viewed as "a horrid evil." The locus of authority was to be Christ as revealed in the New Testament. The reunion of Christendom was to be achieved by the restoration of the New Testament Church. The document reflects Locke's *Letters on Toleration* with overtones of Wycliffe, Meldenius, Stillingfleet, and the Haldanes.

With the establishment of the Brush Run Church June 16, 1811, Alexander Campbell became the leader of the movement in spite of his youth and somewhat controversial inclinations. He was licensed to preach and he continued to do so with increasing power and frequency until his death in 1866. Vachel Lindsay captured the genius of his influence when he wrote:[1]

---

[1]From *Collected Poems,* by Vachel Lindsay, pp. 356-57. Copyright 1923 by The Macmillan Company and used by permission.

He stepped from out the Brush Run Meeting House
To make the big woods his cathedrals,
The river his baptismal font,
The rolling clouds his bells,
The stormy skies his waterfalls,
His pastures and his wells.
Despite all sternness in his word
Richer grew the rushing blood
Within our fathers' coldest thought
Imagination at the flood
Made flowery all they heard.
The deep communion cup
Of the whole South lifted up.

Who were the witnesses, the great cloud of witnesses
With which he was compassed around?
The heroes of faith from the days of Abraham
Stood on the blue-grass ground—
While the battle-ax of thought
Hewed to the bone
That the utmost generation
Till the world was set right
Might have an America their own.
For religion Dionysian
Was far from Campbell's doctrine.

He preached with faultless logic
An American Millennium:
The social order
Of realist and farmer
With every neighbor
Within stone wall and border.
And the tongues of flame came down
Almost in spite of him.

Alexander Campbell must have had a way with women. He called at the home of John Brown, who lived in a substantial farmhouse located on Buffalo Creek just over the Virginia border. John Brown's only daughter, aged 18, looked with an interested eye on the tall Irishman from Washington. Within six months the couple repeated their vows "till death do us part." Within two years Mr. Brown had deeded his farm and home to his son-in-law as an incentive for Alexander to stay in the community rather than take his family to Zanesville, Ohio, where Thomas had moved. Alexander and Margaret soon followed the family custom of founding private schools. In 1818 Buffalo Seminary was in operation. Dorothea Campbell married Joseph Bryant of Washington and stayed in the community. Not to be outdone by her brother, she soon started a seminary for girls at West Middletown, which continued until her death in the latter part of the century. Archibald W. Campbell became a physician in the tri-state area. By midcentury his son, Archibald, Junior, was fighting editor of the *Wheeling Intelligencer*. It was this nephew of Alexander Campbell who called the Convention which made West Virginia a state in 1863. Alexander, however, was the great prophet and public figure of the Campbell family.

In 1829 The Old Dominion called a constitutional convention at Richmond. Some of Campbell's friends urged him to serve as one of the four delegates from the western section of the state. Philip Doddridge of Wellsburg was the natural leader of the Panhandle area. He expressed himself as eager to have Campbell as a colleague. As the canvass for votes began, however, Samuel Sprigg, a Wheeling lawyer, announced that Doddridge backed him against Campbell. This prompted the otherwise reluctant Campbell to fight for the nomination, which he won in a walk. The Convention enabled him to debate the issue of universal white suffrage as against the East Virginian inclination to allow slave owners a substantial political advantage and thus perpetuate themselves in office. The audience for Campbell's political addresses included Chief Justice Marshall, former Presidents James Madison and James Monroe, John Randolph, and Philip Barbour. The west was defeated in the vote which eventually split the state in two. Campbell returned to urge his county to vote against the new constitution which gave political advantage to the slaveholder. Brooke County, where Campbell lived, was the only county unanimous against ratification. This represented, however, only 375 votes. There were only 646 votes in Ohio County which includes Wheeling. Three Ohio county voters favored ratification—slaveholders, no doubt.

Campbell was not only a success at religion and politics. He was a highly successful farmer and businessman. Preaching responsibilities did not keep him from covering the hills with sheep and the meadows with hay. His trading abilities led him into the wool market as a considerable broker. He established a printing press which turned out, first, *The Christian Baptist,* and later, the *Millennial Harbinger,* each of which was a monthly magazine with wide circulation. The press also produced a hymnbook for the churches, which publication returned a handsome profit. He served as postmaster at Bethany, which enabled him to propagate his religious views without expense for postage. He was a shrewd land speculator in a time when values were rapidly increasing. The 1500-acre farm which is now the campus of Bethany College was only a small portion of his vast holdings in several states. In spite of great family expense and major gifts to education and religion, he developed a substantial estate in his lifetime. His boundless energy and natural gifts of eloquence and common sense enabled him to become the world's heavyweight debater with such notable opponents as Robert Owen, the socialist; Bishop Purcell of Cincinnati; and N. L. Rice of Paris, Kentucky. Henry Clay presided at the last of these debates. His popularity as a lecturer carried him to the most celebrated platforms of America. Mark Twain records an amusing episode with reference to his lecture in Hannibal, Missouri.

I have said that Wales was reckless, and he was. It was the recklessness of ever-bubbling and indestructible good spirits flowing from the joy of youth. I think there wasn't anything that that vast boy wouldn't do to procure five minutes' entertainment for himself. One never knew where he would break out next. Among his shining characteristics was the most limitless and adorable irreverence. There didn't seem to be anything serious in life for him; there didn't seem to be anything that he revered.

Once the celebrated founder of the at that time new and widespread sect called Campbellites arrived in our village from Kentucky, and it made a prodigious excitement. The farmers and their families drove or tramped into the village from miles around to get a sight of the illustrious Alexander Campbell and to have a chance to hear him preach. When he preached in a church, many had to be disappointed, for there was no church that would begin to hold all the applicants; so in order to accommodate all, he preached in the open air in the public square, and that was the first time in my life that I had realized what a mighty population this planet contains when you get them all together.

He preached a sermon on one of these occasions which he had written especially for that occasion. All the Campbellites wanted it printed, so that they could save it and read it over and over again, and get it by heart. So they drummed sixteen dollars, which was a large sum then, and for this great sum Mr. Ament contracted to print five hundred copies of that sermon and put them in yellow paper covers. It was a sixteen-page duodecimo pamphlet, and it was a great event in our office. As we regarded it, it was a book, and it promoted us to the dignity of book printers. Moreover, no such mass of actual money as sixteen dollars, in one bunch, had ever entered that office on any previous occasion. People didn't pay for their paper and for their advertising in money; they paid in drygoods, sugar, coffee, hickory wood, oak wood, turnips, pumpkins, onions, watermelons—and it was very seldom indeed that a man paid in money, and when that happened we thought there was something the matter with him.

We set up the great book in pages—eight pages to a form—and by help of a printer's manual we managed to get the pages in their apparently crazy but really sane places on the imposing-stone. We printed that form on a Thursday. Then we set up the remaining eight pages, locked them into a form, and struck a proof. Wales read the proof, and presently was aghast, for he had struck a snag. And it was a bad time to strike a snag, because it was Saturday; it was approaching noon; Saturday afternoon was our holiday, and we wanted to get away and go fishing. At such a time as this Wales struck that snag and showed us what had happened. He had left out a couple of words in a thin-spaced page of solid matter and there wasn't another break-line for two or three pages ahead. What in the world was to be done? Overrun all those pages in order to get in the two missing words? Apparently there was no other way. It would take an hour to do it. Then a revise must be sent to the great minister; we must wait for him to read the revise; if he encountered any errors we must correct them. It looked as if we might lose half the afternoon before we could get away. Then Wales had one of his brilliant ideas. In the line in which the "out" had been made occurred the name Jesus Christ. Wales reduced it in the French way to J. C. It made room for the missing words, but it took 99 per cent of the solemnity out of a particularly solemn sentence. We sent off the revise and waited. We were not intending to wait long. In the circumstances we meant to get out and go fishing before that revise should get back, but we were not speedy enough. Presently that great Alexander Campbell appeared at the far end of that sixty-foot room, and his countenance cast a gloom over the whole place. He strode down to our end and what he said was brief, but it was very stern, and it was to the point. He read Wales a lecture. He said, "So long as you live, don't you ever diminish the Saviour's name again. Put it *all* in." He repeated this admonition a couple of times to emphasize it, then he went away.

In that day the common swearers of the region had a way of their own of *emphasizing* the Saviour's name when they were using it profanely, and this fact intruded itself into Wales' incorrigible mind. It offered him an opportunity for a momentary entertainment which seemed to him to be more precious and more valuable than even fishing and swimming could afford. So he imposed upon himself the long and weary and dreary task of over-running all those long pages in order to improve upon his former work and incidentally and thoughtfully improve upon the great preacher's admonition. He enlarged the offending J. C. into Jesus H. Christ.

Wales knew that that would make prodigious trouble, and it did. But it was not in him to resist it. He had to succumb to the law of his make. I don't remember what his punishment was, but he was not the person to care for that. He had already collected his dividend.[2]

History has a strange way of treating heroes. Daniel Webster, for example, is better known and more honored than he was in his lifetime. Campbell was widely celebrated in his day, but not adequately remembered outside his religious movement in subsequent years. There is today, however, an inclination to recover some of his merited stature. When the work is complete, Campbell will stand forth as a reformer and educator. In the latter capacity he will be best known as the founder of Bethany College, which in turn became the mother of eleven higher institutions, including Texas Christian University in Fort Worth, Butler University in Indianapolis, and Drake University in Des Moines.

The educational views of Campbell deserve considerable review. He launched the *Millennial Harbinger* with the avowed intention of expounding his views on education. His first prospectus, published January 4, 1930, is as follows:

> This work shall be devoted to the destruction of Sectarianism, Infidelity, and Antichristian doctrine and practice. It shall have for its object the development, and introduction of that political and religious order of society called the MILLENNIUM, which will be the consummation of that ultimate amelioration of society proposed in the Christian Scriptures.

Of the specific objectives listed under this, the second one is: "To show the inadequacy of the present systems of education, literary and moral, to develop the powers of the human mind, and to prepare man for rational and social happiness." It is to be noted that his conception was that of a "secular" millennium. The first volume shows his success in carrying out his intention, for in the issue of June 7 he wrote,

---

[2]From *Mark Twain's Autobiography,* Vol. II, reprinted by permission of Harper & Brothers. Copyright 1924, 1952 by Clara Clemens Samossoud.

I have doubted, . . . , for at least fifteen years, whether the present mode of training the human mind in common schools—whether for infants or young men—was not almost antipodes to reason, and sailing against the wind and tide of human nature.

His reason for saying this, he explained, was the fact that "*the natural* sciences, in the present course, are for young men, the last years of their academic, and the *unnatural* sciences . . . are for infants and children!" He further observed, "More than half the time spent in the collegiate way was lost, . . . which might, under a rational system, be obtained at the age of from sixteen to eighteen."

Editorials and printed addresses in early issues gave much attention to educational matters. He was of the firm conviction that the only way in which common-school teaching could be reformed was by improvement in the colleges where teachers are trained. He gave hearty approval to the diatribes of Thomas Smith Grimke of South Carolina who launched a verbal campaign against devotion to Greece and Rome in higher education. He contended that schools should have more regard for current affairs and less for the classics. His conception of education as outlined in these early comments revealed two fundamental principles which influenced all his subsequent thought: namely, that education should begin in infancy and last all through a lifetime; and, second, that it should be for everyone. In the year 1840 this interest led him to the founding of Bethany College. He set aside $15,000 of his own money for the enterprise, assembled a few well-trained men, procured a charter, and made ready to begin instruction. The new institution was to present

a system of education founded upon all the demands of our nature in the ratio of their importance, developing a human being to himself, his physical, intellectual, and moral constitution—his position in the universe, and corresponding obligations and duties—his capacities and sources of enjoyment, inducting him into those sciences and moral habits essential to his usefulness and true excellence.

He further described the purpose of the institution by saying,

It is intended to lay a broad, as well as a deep and permanent foundation for eminent usefulness in every department of Bethany College. For this purpose it is contemplated to have a very liberal and extensive course of scientific studies—and to give to the sciences, both physical and mental, a space proportioned to their relative value and importance in the intellectual and moral development and improvement of the human faculties.

The first teaching staff consisted of A. F. Ross from New Athens College, Ohio, professor of ancient languages and ancient history; Charles Stuart of Kentucky, professor of algebra and general mathematics; R. Richardson, professor of chemistry, geology, and the kindred sciences; W. K. Pendleton, of the University of Virginia, professor of natural philosophy "and such of the natural sciences as come not in the course of Dr. R. Richardson." The president himself was to teach mental philosophy, evidences of Christianity, morals, and political economy. A sixth man was to be added, as a professor of English literature, and as many tutors as were needed. Of this faculty, Mr. Campbell said they are "mostly young men under thirty years of age, of highly respectable attainments, of much force of character, of exemplary morals, and ardent devotion to science, literature, and the advancement of education."

The college was founded as a liberal arts institution. While Campbell was eager to train ministers for the rapidly multiplying churches, he was interested also in the education of men for the secular vocations. His appeal to the churches for support in the *Millennial Harbinger* of June, 1841, reads:

Popular education is dependent on liberal education, as lakes and rivers are dependent on oceans and seas for their periodical and full supplies. The Family, the State, the Church, with a hundred voices demand a number of such institutions as that in contemplation. And can we not, friends of humanity, civilization, morality, and religion, that we are—I say, can we not, shall we not, erect and establish one or two such institutions, and thus contribute our mite to the advancement of the great cause of human redemption from ignorance, immorality, superstition, and error!

Campbell understood the liberal arts as follows:

They are called liberal arts and sciences, not merely because they free the human mind from vulgar prejudices, ignorance, and error which they certainly do; but because they are general in their character and application, and open to us an extensive acquaintance with literature, science, and art; and thus furnish us with the means of extending our acquaintance with nature, society, and the Bible, to any extent commensurate with the wants of our nature and the limits of our existence.[3]

The scheme of the curriculum was much like that of the University of Virginia. Campbell was an admirer of Thomas Jefferson and was undoubtedly familiar with the work of the great school which was the pride of Jefferson. It is not surprising that the University of Virginia afforded its share of Bethany's first faculty. The school of sacred history and moral philosophy required four years for its completion and included such studies as the evidences of Christianity, sacred history, biblical literature, ecclesiastical history, and moral philosophy. Over this school the president himself presided. There was also a school of mathematics and astronomy which required three years for completion and had a rich offering of algebra, geometry, trigonometry, surveying, astronomy, etc. The early announcements clearly indicate the purpose of these studies which was

the development of the intellectual powers, the formation and cultivation of correct habits of thought and investigation, but a rigid regard to the logic and philosophy of mathematics, are made the paramount object of every recitation. Freedom of thought and inquiry, in harmony with the laws of analysis and synthesis, is encouraged; original modes of demonstration are highly estimated in the grading of scholarship, and every proper stimulus is employed to inspire in the student a generous love of science.[4]

---

[3]*Millennial Harbinger,* 1849, p. 433.
[4]Ibid., 1855, p. 227.

The school of natural, intellectual, and political philosophy could be completed in two years. This corresponded to what we call physics and social science, and included psychology in addition to political economy and government. It is commendable that this pioneer educator made efforts to equip the school with the best possible laboratory, of which he said:

> Nature is presented as she seems to the senses, and her phenomena explained in the language and to the comprehension of the popular mind. For this purpose the institution is provided with an extensive philosophical apparatus, affording the means of experimental demonstration of all the leading and more interesting phenomena of this department of science.[5]

His interest in American government led him to include courses in constitutional and international law. Of this he said, "In no country on the globe is it so important that every citizen should understand the great and fundamental principles of government, as in America, and yet the study of these has, hitherto, been almost totally neglected in the literary institutions of our country."[6] A two-year course was also offered in chemistry and belles lettres. The chemical division was prepared to offer laboratory studies to supplement the lectures and textbooks. The applied aspects of the study of physiology and agriculture were specifically mentioned in the aims of the course. The department of belles lettres within this school was the customary literary course. A preparatory school and a school of Hebrew and modern languages completed the curricular offering. It is interesting to compare this arrangement of studies into seven schools with the eight schools which made up the curriculum of the University of Virginia at its beginning in 1825. In that catalogue were presented (1) the ancient languages, (2) the modern languages, (3) mathematics, (4) natural philosophy, (5) natural history, (6) medicine, (7) moral philosophy, (8) law. The

---

[5] p. 228.
[6] p. 229.

influence of Thomas Jefferson on Campbell would make an interesting study. He spoke of the work of Jefferson as "the emancipation of the human mind from the shackles of superstition." He made frequent reference to the University of Virginia in his addresses, and in describing the "bill of fare" offered at the Stewards Inn, where the students were boarded, he said that the food diet was that which was offered at the University of Virginia. In keeping with the practice of that school, he permitted the student to elect schools and even certain courses. Modern languages and Hebrew were offered on an elective basis. This is significant because the general idea of election had not yet been accepted.

The hallmark of Bethany education, according to its founder, was to be "man's recognition of his responsibility to carry on the great American institutions, such as the school, the church, the state, the home, and the professions." He, therefore, demanded that all academic procedure be in accord with "the genius of humanity and the wants of society." In an apostrophe to the college, he said:

> Men, and not brick and mortar, make colleges, and these colleges make men. These men make books, and these books make the living world in which we individually live, and move, and have our being. How all-important, then, that our colleges should understand and teach the true philosophy of man! They create the men that furnish the teachers of men—the men that fill the pulpit, the legislative halls, the senators, the judges and the governors of earth. Do we expect to fill these high stations by merely voting or praying for men? Or shall we choose empirics, charlatans, mountebanks, and every pretender to eminent claims upon the suffrages of the people? Forbid it, reason, conscience, and Heaven!

The influence of this stalwart reformer and educator still lives in the churches and schools which his genius developed. His 1,500-acre farm is now the campus of Bethany College. His old home is becoming an American shrine to take its place with Monticello and Mt. Vernon. America is beginning to realize that here in these tumbled mountains a Scotch-Irish immigrant inspired institutions and influences which have a significant bearing on the destiny of Western civilization. An admiring poet sensed this fact before the historians began their deliberate work:

> Let a thousand Prophets have their due
> Let each have his boat in the sky
> But you were born for his secular millennium
> With the old Kentucky forest blooming like heaven,
> And the redbirds flying high.[7]

---

[7] Lindsay, *op. cit.*

The Age of Alexander Campbell

ARTHUR SCHLESINGER, JR.

Associate Professor of History at Harvard University and author of the Pulitzer prize-winning volume, **The Age of Jackson**

When Alexander Campbell first arrived in the United States on September 29, 1809, he found a nation in a state of spectacular growth. The area of the country had almost doubled in the decade before his disembarkation in New York, and the population had increased nearly 40 per cent. Society was everywhere on the move. People were pressing restlessly into the West, seeking new homes on the ever-receding frontier. A growing fluidity of life was marked on the East as well. The old class distinctions were beginning to break down; the knee breeches, ruffled shirts, cocked hats, and wigs of the past were beginning to disappear. Democratizing forces, accumulating in the course of the 18th century, released during the War for Independence, renewed by the excitements of the election of 1800 and by the pull of Westward expansion, were giving the nation new expectations and new values. Nor could anything hope to escape the democratizing process—not politics, nor literature, nor even religion itself.

The democratic mood was composed of many elements. Perhaps most basic was the new estimate, emerging over the last two centuries, of the worth and possibility of the ordinary individual, not only as a soul to be saved, but equally as a being deserving happiness during his passage on earth. From this new focus much else followed. A heightened faith in individual dignity was leading to the assertion of man's right to acquire and judge for himself. A heightened concern for the individual personality was leading to the conviction that "the pursuit of happiness" was a proper human goal. A heightened respect for individual enterprise was leading to the sense that the interests of all were best served by indulging the interests of each. A heightened faith in individual reason was leading to the growing commitment to the methods and objectives of natural science. The new individualism was, above all, rationalistic and optimistic; it expected the universe to be intelligible, and it expected it to be kind. If democracy was the politics of the new individualism, then humanitarianism was its ethics, capitalism its economics, and science increasingly its cosmology.

Yet the democratic mood clashed with much of the past—not alone with the politics of George III and the economies of mercantilism but also with the theology of John Calvin. For, in its most severe form, Calvinism relentlessly challenged basic presuppositions of democratic individualism. Its belief in total depravity contradicted the new faith in natural reason. Its belief in foreordination, election, and eternal punishment affronted the new humanitarian ideas of justice. Its belief in imputation and hereditary guilt was incompatible with the new faith in personal merit and demerit. Its belief in dogmatic theology conflicted with the new assertion of the right of private judgment. Its predisposition in favor of strict ecclesiastical discipline offended democratic notions of social organization. Above all, Calvinism pursued happiness in the next world, not in this, and for the Supreme Deity, not for vile and corrupt man. In an important sense Calvinism was both irrational and pessimistic. It did not expect the universe to conform to human notions of justice and reasonableness; nor did it expect man's travel, either now or hereafter, to be sweet and easy.

II

The contrast between the old Calvinism and the new democratic individualism was bound to set up strains. It did so, and on fundamental levels. Young men and women, growing up in the new mood, found the old faith harder and harder to accept. It was not only that Calvinism was unreasonable; more important, perhaps, was the fact that it was unbearable. The demands it made, not on just human reason but on the human sensibility, were too appalling to be endured. Consider for a moment the testimony of those born in the last years of the 18th century.

Horace Mann, born in 1796:

> In the way in which they [the Calvinist doctrines] came to my youthful mind, a certain number of souls were to be forever lost, and nothing—not powers, nor principalities, nor man, nor angel, nor Christ, nor the Holy Spirit, nay, not God himself—could save them; for he had sworn before time was, to get eternal glory out of their eternal torment. . . . Like all children, I believed what I was taught. To my vivid imagination, a physical hell was a living reality, as much so as though I could have heard the shrieks of the tormented, or stretched out my hand to grasp their burning

souls, in a vain endeavor for their rescue. Such a faith spread a pall of blackness over the whole heavens, shutting out every beautiful and glorious thing. . . . Often, on going to bed at night, did the objects of the day and the faces of friends give place to a vision of the awful throne, the inexorable Judge, and the hapless myriads, among whom I often seemed to see those whom I loved best; and there I wept and sobbed until Nature found that counterfeit repose in exhaustion.[1]

John A. Dix, born in 1798:

I derived no agreeable impression whatever from these religious observances . . . My mother's affectionate teachings had implanted within me grains of devotion which time could not fail to bring forth and ripen. But her God never seemed to me the same Deity who was worshipped at the meeting-house. Hers was all goodness and mercy and pardoning love; while the other seemed to me a severe master, burning with anger at the impenitence of the human race.[2]

Catherine Beecher, born in 1800:

I then felt I was created a miserable, helpless creature; that I and all my fellow-men were placed under a severe law which we were *naturally* unable to obey, and threatened with everlasting despair for violating *one* of its precepts.[3]

William H. Seward, born in 1801:

The first mental anxiety which I recall was, manifestly, an effect of the fearful presentation of death and its consequences, so common in the sermons and exhortations of the clergy at that day . . . I often was watchful at night, through fear that if I should fall asleep I should awake in the consuming flame which was appointed as a discipline that allows no reformation . . . Reflecting upon this incident, it became an interesting study afterward, how constantly

---

[1]Mary P. Mann, *Life of Horace Mann* (Boston, 1865), 13-15.

[2]From *Memoirs* of *John Adams Dix,* compiled by Morgan Dix, Harper & Brothers, 1883, pp. 15, 17.

[3]Letter from Catherine Beecher to Lyman Beecher, January 1, 1823, Lyman Beecher, in *Autobiography, Correspondence, Etc.* (New York, 1864), I, 497.

a decline of imaginary terrors in the future state of being attends the progress of mankind in natural science.[4]

A faith which had seemed stern common sense in an earlier century was now beginning to appear, in the words of the editor Joseph T. Buckingham, "a piece of gratuitous and unprofitable cruelty." "My whole mind rebelled against this teaching," said the young Benjamin F. Butler. "I could not and did not believe it." Dr. Oliver Wendell Holmes argued that Calvinism, consistently accepted, could only end in madness. John Quincy Adams, hearing a minister quote Isaac Watts's view that men were more base and brutish than the beasts, reflected, "If Watts had said this on a weekday to any one of his parishioners, would he not have knocked him down? And how can that be taught as a solemn truth of religion, applicable to all mankind, which, if said at any other time to any one individual, would be punishable as slander?" God, it was Adams' creed, "will not suffer us to do evil, and then sentence us severely for what He has suffered us to do. My reason and my sense of justice will not yield to any other creed than this."

III

The reason and the sense of justice of a whole generation were at stake. The emotions experienced by the youthful Manns and Dixes, Catherine Beechers and Sewards, multiplied a thousandfold, could result only in an invincible distaste for the unacceptable doctrines. With this distaste there came in many cases a turning away from the churches themselves; for the insistence on maintaining the old dogma in its harshness as a qualification for membership was making communion increasingly difficult. The total number of communicants in 1800 was less than 400,000—an average of one for about every 14.5

[4]From *William H. Seward, an Autobiography* (Derby and Miller, 1877), 22-23.

persons in the country (as compared to one for every 1.6 persons claimed today.)[5] The very incidence of revivalism was itself a symptom of a situation where people combined a great anxiety to believe with a great inability to accept prevailing doctrine. The characteristic cycle from spiritual "deadness" to revivalist ecstasy to "backsliding" revealed a condition of apathy, occasionally energized by guilt into a frenzy of belief, but soon relapsing into the original indifference.

In such conditions, it was inevitable that people imbued with the democratic spirit should begin to revise the unacceptable doctrines in accordance with the new standards of justice and reasonableness. It was inevitable, too, that they should rebel against authoritarian forms of church polity. As Americans had already declared independence in politics, so at the end of the 18th and start of the 19th centuries Americans began to declare independence in religion. And, as the attempt to narrow the gap between political theory and the people had produced an extraordinary burst of political creativity, so the attempt to narrow the gap between theology and the people now brought about a great release of invention and energy in the field of religion.

The democratic impulse emphasized individual judgment and individual initiative. It was this impulse, for example, which led young Barton Warren Stone in the late 1790's to revolt against the severe Presbyterianism of his youth. The Presbyterian God professed great love for his children, Stone said, but then gave them commands which could not be obeyed and punished them for disobedience; such a God, he wrote, "no rational creature can love or honor. . . . What man acting thus would not be despised as a monster, or demon in human shape, and

[5]See *Problem of Religious Progress,* by Daniel Dorchester, 1881, pp. 540, 545. For contemporary estimates, see, for example, *Dr. George Gallup's 1956 Pocket Almanac of Facts,* p. 70. Two points should be made, however, about these statistics. In the first place, all religious statistics are unreliable; and, in the second place, the statistics of 1790 were based on actual communicants, while contemporary statistics are generally based on loose definitions, including, for example, baptized infants as church members.

be hissed from all respectable society?" If rational man were the measure of God, then Calvinism had to be rejected. As Stone later put it, "Calvinism is among the heaviest clogs on Christianity in the world. It is a dark mountain between heaven and earth, and is amongst the most discouraging hindrances to sinners from seeking the kingdom of God."[6] And, where the democratic impulse moved Stone to challenge dogma, it led a young Methodist minister, James O'Kelly, to challenge polity. Rising against the episcopal organization of Methodism, O'Kelly formed a new group whose name testified to its character. They called themselves "Republican Methodists," a plain assertion that the church was as necessary a field for republicanization as society itself.

IV

Stone and O'Kelly were only two of many men responding to the tensions between Calvinism and democracy by new religious departures; but they were men whose experiments were especially relevant, of course, to the story of Alexander Campbell. When Campbell himself arrived in America a few years later, he found the democratizing process even further advanced. And he himself had already in his native Scotland begun to respond to the same tensions between Calvinism and the new spirit—a fact which should caution those too easily inclined to interpret the rise of the Christian Churches as the by-product of religion on the frontier. Long before he ever saw the American wilderness, Campbell's recoil from the ecclesiastical organization of the Scottish Presbyterians had given him a belief in independency in church polity. And the spreading faith in human capacity—as vital in Britain and France as in Kentucky and Tennessee—had already raised doubts in his mind concerning the rigid fatalism of the older Calvinism.

[6]*The Biography of Eld. Barton Warren Stone, Written by Himself,* p. 33.

Yet Campbell was also uneasily aware that the surge toward private judgment in dogma and independency in organization was creating problems. In particular, these tendencies had accelerated a rush toward sectarianism which obviously conflicted with the universalist aspirations of Christianity. Alexander Campbell and his father, reared in the intense atmosphere of Scottish theological disputation, with Seceders, Burghers, Anti-Burghers, Old Light Burghers, New Light Burghers and all the rest, had a peculiar detestation for what Thomas Campbell called "the bitter jarrings and janglings of a party spirit." When they came to America, they found that their remarks on this theme provoked a heartening response. For their dislike of what they called "partyism" in religion had much in common with George Washington's warning in his Farewell Address against the "baneful effects of the spirit of party" in politics. Division among Christians, said Campbell's *Declaration and Address* of the Christian Association, was "a horrid evil," anti-Christian, antiscriptural, antinatural, "productive of confusion and of every evil work." When the Campbells proposed to bring peace and unity to religion, they expressed aspirations highly congenial to the new democratic faith which, for all its individualism, nonetheless conceived society as uniform and homogeneous. "The appearance of party is a beacon proclaiming a tendency, which instantly alarms despotism," John Taylor of Caroline had said; ". . . . General, and not party opinion, is the principle of our policy."

The Campbells thus confronted a dilemma on their arrival in the United States. On the one hand, the old religion had lost much of its relevance to people's needs and hopes; on the other, agitated attempts to restore that relevance had produced only a confusion of clamoring sects. The need was plainly to restate the Christian faith in terms which would appeal to people's sense of reason and justice, as Calvinism no longer did—but, at the same time, to do this in a way which, instead of promoting partyism, might provide even a stronger basis for Christian unity than the Westminster Confession. It was to this great task that the Campbells now dedicated themselves.

V

What did the new democratic spirit seek of theology? Against the old belief in abstruse and complex doctrine, it insisted on simplicity and intelligibility. Against the old belief in dogmatic and binding creeds, it affirmed the right of private judgment. It wanted a God of mercy, not a God of wrath; and it saw the individual, not as a helpless instrument of unpredictable divine grace, but as a man capable of making his own contribution toward salvation. And, while in the last resort it gave priority to the right of private judgment, it still yearned for a rebirth of Christian unity.

The Campbells expressed this democratic spirit with great fidelity. Though the elder Campbell's health had been the immediate reason for their migration to the United States, the decision came in an atmosphere when many of their fellow countrymen, confronting dispiriting economic and political prospects in Scotland, were avowedly seeking better opportunities in the American democracy. After seven years in the United States Alexander Campbell wrote a relative in Scotland,

> "I cannot speak too highly of the advantages that the people in this country enjoy in being delivered from a proud and lordly aristocracy; and here it becomes very easy to trace the common national evils of all European countries to their proper source, and chiefly to that first germ of oppression, of civil and religious tyranny. . . . I would not exchange the honor and privilege of being an American citizen for the position of your king."[7]

The nature of their audience confirmed their democratic convictions. Addressing predominantly Scotch-Irish congrega-

[7]From *Memoirs of Alexander Campbell,* by Robert Richardson, I, 465-466.

tions in western Pennsylvania and western Virginia, they were appealing to the hardy and self-reliant small farmers, shopkeepers, and workers whose aspirations would help bring about the Jacksonian revolution. "The chief priests, the scribes and the rulers of the people are generally in league against us," wrote Campbell almost in Jacksonian terms, recalling his tours of the eighteen twenties. As late as 1839, describing his communicants in the South, he wrote, "We have a few educated intelligent men, as we have a few rich and powerful; but the majority are poor, ignorant and uneducated."

Why had religion lost contact with the rising democracy? One trouble, the Campbells felt, was the extent to which essential religion had been overlaid through the centuries with man-made speculation. The substitution of creeds for faith, as they saw it, was the source of authoritarianism, of factionalism, and of unintelligibility. Soon after coming to America, Thomas Campbell protested against "the introduction of human opinions and human inventions into the faith and worship of the Church"; and Alexander Campbell repeatedly depreciated "the unauthorized though consecrated jargon on trinity, unity, atonement, sacrifice, etc., etc." The only sure footing the Campbells could discern in this tumult of dogma was the Bible itself; thus Thomas Campbell's dictum: "WHERE THE SCRIPTURES SPEAK, WE SPEAK; AND WHERE THE SCRIPTURES ARE SILENT, WE ARE SILENT." And Scriptures meant, above all, the New Testament. "Outside of the apostolic canon," said Alexander Campbell, "there is not, as it appears to me, one solid foot of terra firma on which to raise the superstructure ecclesiastic." "We neither advocate," he said on another occasion, "Calvinism, Arminianism, Socinianism, Arianism, Trinitarianism, Unitarianism, Deism nor Sectarianism, but *New Testamentism.*"

In these terms they sought to clear away the sophistications which encrusted the biblical faith and to uncover an unassailable basis for Christian unity in New Testament primitivism. For

Campbell the apostolic days had somewhat the role that the primeval state of nature had for Locke—whom Campbell so much admired—a moment of historical purity which could serve ever after as the measure of the rights and duties of man. Political liberalism in the 18th century thought more of the past than of the future; its predominant impulse was to re-vindicate ancient rights rather than to vindicate new ones. Campbell's theology reflected this impulse of nostalgia—the yearning for a primitive state where, in Locke's words,

being all equip and independent, no one ought to harm another in his life, health, liberty or possessions; for men being all the workmanship of one omnipotent and infinitely wise Maker; all the servants of one sovereign master, sent into the world by His order and about His business; they are His property, whose workmanship they are made to last during His, not one another's pleasure.[8]

Campbell's attack on the obfuscations of theology had certain resemblance too to the contemporary attacks of Jacksonian reformers on the obfuscations of the common law. As codification would reduce the authority of judges and introduce stability into law, so New Testamentism would reduce the authority of ministers and introduce stability into religion. In each case there was a desire to render the subject accessible to the common man and thus to cut the ground from under the privileged class—whether of priests or of judges—who had held power through their vested interests in obscurity.

Nor was this search for definiteness incompatible with the right of private judgment; it was, indeed, the process which validated that right. The essential distinction was between "faith"—that is, "the Bible, the whole Bible, and nothing but the Bible"—and "opinion." "While we earnestly contend for the faith," said Alexander Campbell, "to allow perfect freedom of opinion and of the expression of opinion, is the true philosophy

[8]*An Essay Concerning the True Original Extent and End of Civil Government*, chapter 2.

of church union and the sovereign antidote against heresy." Men, in other words, should "leave the conscience free where God has left it free." On occasion, he made the comparison with republican society explicit. "Civil rulers have no right to tolerate or punish men on account of their opinions in matters of religion. Neither have Christians a right to condemn their brethren for difference of opinion." Little could be worse than insistence on dogma. "When men make communion in religious worship dependent on uniformity of opinion," Campbell said, "they make self-love, instead of the love of God, the bond of union."

VI

In this manner, Campbell sought to make faith more intelligible and more definite, providing a basis for unity while at the same time strengthening the right of private judgment. But the simplification of faith was only part of the process of democratization. Another part was the humanization of faith—the transformation of Christianity from a hopeless contest between a severe and all-powerful Deity and corrupt and impotent man to a constructive collaboration between rational man and a solicitous God.

The process of humanization had many aspects. Thus the fall of man lost for Campbell its decisive importance in the divine economy; original sin became a chronic human tendency rather than a state of total and constitutional depravity. The atonement now proceeded out of the mercy of God rather than out of his offended sense of justice. God himself somewhat receded in Campbell's scheme, and Christ assumed a new and central significance. When Campbell spoke of Christian unity, he meant, without derogation to God, unity around Christ—"Christ alone being the *head,* the centre; his word the *rule,* and explicit belief of and manifest conformity to it in all things, the *terms*." Or, as Isaac Errett summed it up, "We therefore urge the Word of God against human creeds; faith in Christ against faith in systems of theology; obedience to Christ after than obedience to church authority; the Church of Christ in place of sects."

The orientation of faith around Christ expressed the shift in interest from sin to salvation. Perhaps the most striking of Campbell's theological innovations (or, as he would have said, "restorations") was his reconsideration of the processes of salvation. This reconsideration revolved particularly around the meaning of baptism—the question which entangled Campbell in some of his sharpest controversies and which, as much as any other, compelled him against his first inclination to found a communion of his own. The problem of baptism had many aspects. Much of the controversy—for example, the argument about "sprinkling" versus "immersion"—followed from Campbell's effort to perform the baptismal rite as closely as possible in the manner of the primitive church. But the aspect of baptism relevant here was Campbell's reinterpretation of the rite in terms which gave new scope in the pursuit of salvation to human initiative and human self-esteem.

For the older Calvinists, acceptance into communion required an unmistakable and convulsive religious experience. The pretense or illusion of belief was not enough, for sinners were by definition incapable of authentic belief; they required first a shattering sense of illumination by the spirit of God—an experience of physical reconstitution and regeneration which alone could make faith possible. For many who believed in God, the failure to have such a conclusive verification of faith was the cause of great guilt and tribulation. Barton W. Stone, recalling his youthful search for regeneration, later wrote, "For one year I was tossed on the waves of uncertainty—laboring, praying, and striving to obtain saving faith—sometimes desponding, and almost despairing of ever getting it." When preachers "labored to arouse me from my torpor by the terrors of God, and the horrors of hell," Stone could only sink into "an indescribable apathy." Indeed the demand for a prolonged inner upheaval as a prerequisite to conversion was an important factor in producing the contagion of religious apathy at the end of the 18th century.

VII

If a man felt he believed in God and wanted to join a church but still could not achieve the experience of regeneration, either he was condemned to the cycle of anguish and apathy, or else he might attempt a personal break-through of his own to faith. Thus Stone at last found resolution by yielding to the non-Calvinist conviction that God was love, that Christ had come to seek and save the lost. "I now saw," he wrote, "that a poor sinner was as much authorized to believe in Jesus at first, as at last"—as much at the beginning of the process of conversion, that is, as at the end—"that *now* was the accepted time, and day of salvation."

Alexander Campbell himself had come to religion in Scotland in a similar manner. After a period of struggle, he was enabled to put his trust in the Savior and feel his reliance on him: "It never entered into my head," he later wrote, "to investigate the subject of baptism or the doctrines of the creed." In the United States, like Stone, he now vigorously condemned the thesis that protracted internal agony was a condition precedent to the capacity for faith. He sharply rejected the view, as he put it, "that a sinner is so dead and buried in his sin, that even after he has heard the voice of God, speaking by Apostles and Prophets, he must wait still for the Spirit to descend and work faith in his heart by a supernatural process before he attempt even to call upon the name of the Lord."[9] For Campbell—and

[9] *Millennial Harbinger,* 1837, p. 198.

for the primitive church, as he read Scriptures—faith simply meant belief in testimony. If a person accepted the evidence of Scriptures, if he confessed his faith in Christ, he qualified, without further ado, for communion and salvation. His own decision was essential; he did not have to wait in torment for the visitation of the Holy Spirit. In short, Campbell regarded faith, repentance, baptism, and the remission of sins as possible *before* the regeneration wrought by the Holy Spirit; while, for the older Calvinists, nothing was possible until *after* the months of questioning, doubt, terror, and the final illumination.

What Campbell, Stone, and the others thus contended was that even sinners were capable of believing the testimony of the Bible, of acting upon it, of coming to Christ, of obeying him, and then of obtaining from him salvation and the Holy Spirit. Against this view, Calvinism, in Campbell's judgment, divested "man of every attribute that renders him accountable to his Maker, and assimilates all his actions to the bending of the trees or the tumults of the ocean occasioned by the tempest." As Stone later wrote, "When we first began to preach these things, the people appeared as just awakened from the sleep of ages—they seemed to see for the first time that they were responsible beings." *Human responsibility* was the key. Men were no longer impotent before God; they could do things of their own initiative to bring themselves into the area of salvation, and they could do them forthwith. No one with access to Scriptures, Campbell said, had any excuse for unbelief and unregeneracy; "Those who have put on the Lord Jesus are invited to abound in all the joys, consolations and purifying influences of this Holy Spirit."

VIII

The democratization of religion involved more than the simplification and humanization of theology. It also involved a reconsideration of the problems of church organization. Here again Campbell turned to the New Testament for guidance; but here again his proposals expressed the democratic temper of the times. The Christian Churches were growing as a result of self-organization and self-determination. Stone and his followers came to the new movement from the Presbyterians, the "Republican Methodists" from Methodism, others from Baptism. Campbell and the Disciples offered a congregational polity on democratic lines, in which each church was independent and each congregation chose and ordained its own officers. So mistrustful was he of ecclesiastical organization that, for a time, he objected to missionary, education, and Bible societies and even to Sunday schools.

This mistrust carried over to the clergy itself. As the Jacksonian uprising had an anti-intellectual strain, leaving in its trail a scorn for lawyers and for scholars, so Campbell for many years had little use for the professional clergy. Preachers seemed to him a collection of clerical operators, raising people's admiration of themselves for their own advantage, scheming to make more money and gain more influence, committed to bigotry, sectarianism, and obscurantism. "As a body of men," he wrote, "they have taken away the key of knowledge from the people." The Campbells could find nothing in Scriptures making a "high degree of doctrinal information" necessary for salvation: "the church from the beginning did and ever will, consist of little children and young men, as well as fathers." Alexander Campbell's own mission, as he saw it, was democratic and militant—it was "to take the New Testament out of the abuses of the clergy and put it into the hands of the people."

There was in all this an element, as Henry Adams suggested, of calling on the church to "ignore what it could not comprehend," as if intellectual difficulties must be inessential because they were insuperable. But Jacksonian Democracy, while resenting what seemed to it the arrogance of the educated, placed a high value on education itself. So too did Campbell, who fought for many years for the principle of free public education and set up a school of his own, Buffalo Seminary, as early as 1818. Bethany College has remained, of course, the great monument to Alexander Campbell's faith in education. Campbell's growing concern for education and, in time, even for a trained ministry resulted no doubt in part from the needs of the Christian Churches, as soon as they were established as a separate denomination; it resulted too perhaps from the rising social status and expectations of the members of the Christian movement. But it testified more basically to Campbell's own deep faith in education as—in his Baccalaureate Address of 1853—"one of the chief bulwarks of religion, morality, and representative government."

Yet his eventful acceptance of a professional clergy did not diminish his abhorrence for the whole idea of the clergy as a privileged group or for the notion of established churches. He praised the United States as "a country happily exempted from the baneful influence of a civil establishment of any peculiar form of Christianity." When Ezra Stiles Ely, a Presbyterian minister, proposed "*a Christian party in politics,*" Campbell denounced him; and he strongly supported Richard M. Johnson's report rejecting the Sabbatarian attempt to stop the Sunday mails—so strongly, indeed, as to give rise to an unsubstantiated tradition that he was the report's author. Though Campbell carried his belief in the separation of church and state to the point of virtually ignoring the politics of the day ("I know of nothing more antipodal to the gospel than politics"), he was nonetheless expressing a predominant Jacksonian mood in his opposition to the political presumptions of the churches.[10]

[10]Richardson, *op. cit.*, I, 253; see also Lunger, *Political Ethics of Alexander Campbell*, chapters 3, 4; Arthur M. Schlesinger, Jr., *The Age of Jackson* (Boston, 1945), chapters 11, 27. Dr. Lunger points out that Campbell did not carry his belief in separation to the point of objecting to the establishment in his home of a post office bringing with it certain franking privileges.

The problems of the millennial enthusiasms of the day require further study; but no one can doubt a relationship between social conditions and the millennial dream. A belief in the millennium has been a characteristic faith of the disinherited. In certain respects, the establishment of utopian communities in the United States in these years represented a secularization of the millennial hope. Though Campbell himself was always a cautious millenarian, nonetheless he named his magazine the *Millennial Harbinger* and plainly believed that the millennium was impending. "The Millennium," he declared in 1841,

> will be a state of greatly enlarged and continuous prosperity, in which the Lord will be exalted and his divine spirit enjoyed in an unprecedented measure. All the conditions of society will be vastly improved; wars shall cease, and peace and good will among men will generally abound . . . Crimes and punishments will cease; governments will recognize human rights . . . the seasons will become more mild; climates more salubrious, health more vigorous, labor less, lands more fertile, and the animal creation more prolific.[11]

The very language is reminiscent of contemporary predictions of Albert Brisbane and other disciples of Fourier.

IX

If Campbell expressed many of the aspirations of American democracy in the Jacksonian period, he expressed, too, his share of its confusions. His most conspicuous failure perhaps was his hesitation to come to grips with the moral challenge of slavery. While he was nominally in favor of abolition and had a vivid sense of the demoralizing consequences of the slavery system, he nonetheless could see no Christian reason to affirm the evil of slave-holding. Slavery, he lamely concluded, was inexpedient

[11]p. 9.

but not immoral. This equivocation may have been prompted in part by the explosive character of the issue for a church with many members in slave territory. But perhaps it came more profoundly from his reluctance to apply Christianity to any social or political problems.

Campbell's long campaign against the Roman Catholic Church expressed another of the less appealing aspects of the mass democracy of the day. While Campbell refrained on the whole from the cheap anti-Catholicism of the know-nothing type, he denounced Catholicism as "essentially anti-American, being opposed to the genius of all free institutions, and positively subversive of them." Actually his own theology, with its emphasis on freedom of opinion, offered a formula for religious pluralism in America. Campbell underestimated the extent to which a vital pluralism could absorb even a faith with the universalist aspirations of Roman Catholicism.

These lapses of clear-sightedness were perhaps part of the somewhat literal and legalistic cast of mind which Campbell sometimes brought to religion—and here again he was typical of tendencies in the democracy of his time. Tocqueville, visiting America in the 1830's, observed that the language of the law

had become in some measure a vulgar tongue;

the spirit of the Law, which is produced in the schools and courts of justice, gradually penetrates beyond their walls into the bosom of society, where it descends to the lowest classes, so that at last the whole people contract the habits and the tastes of the judicial magistrate.[12]

Campbell's effort to solve all problems by invoking words of the New Testament with the naïve belief that these words required no particular interpretation encouraged a verbalistic attention to the letter of the law, sometimes—as in the case of slavery—at the clear expense of the spirit. And, as Dr. Lunger

[12]*Democracy in America,* by Alexis de Tocqueville (vintage edition), I, 290.

has pointed out, Campbell concentrated on the Acts and Epistles rather than on the Gospels and the Sermon on the Mount. This emphasis further deprived his faith of the prophetic quality—the sense of tension between history and eternity—responsible for the more penetrating moral insights.

Yet Campbell, in his very lack of irony and tragedy, was once again faithful to the democratic mood of his times. These were days of expansion and hope, and they required a reinterpretation of religion. The sterile and mechanical pessimism of the older Calvinism, while retaining the language of tragedy, did not have, in any high sense, the tragic spirit; it was without the vitality to adjust to the new age. A group of religious pioneers attempted to exercise in adjustment. Because they were men of moral sensitivity and religious devotion, they sought earnestly to preserve the essence of the Christian tradition as they understood it. Because they loved their nation and their fellow Americans, and because they believed profoundly in human dignity and reason, they sought to have religion recognize the capacities and aspirations of the people. Among these men, Alexander Campbell, by his high-mindedness, his generosity, and his serenity, occupies a leading place. His theology and his life display his success in accommodating religion to the spirit of the times while keeping the sense of vantage points beyond history without which religion would lose its meaning.

Pioneer in Broadcloth

WINFRED E. GARRISON

Professor of Philosophy at the University of Houston and author of **Religion Follows the Frontier,** *as well as several standard works in church history*

The contrasting coloration of the two principal words in the title, "Pioneer in Broadcloth," is intentional. It assumes, of course, that the reference is to the historical rather than to the contemporary kind of broadcloth. It once had a connotation of dignity which it does not carry in its current use. Now we buy a shirt of so-called broadcloth for three or four dollars. The material is a smooth-textured white cotton and it makes a good enough shirt, but such "broadcloth" adds nothing to our social status. In the days of our fathers—or of our great-grandfathers, depending on the point of reference—broadcloth was the heavy and lustrous woolen fabric from which merchant tailors fashioned the black, skirted coats that were the formal habiliments of gentlemen, especially of preachers but also of politicians and of any who could make plausible pretensions to gentility. That such garments of such cloth also became the uniform of professional gamblers on the "floating palaces" that plied the Ohio and Mississippi was, like other forms of hypocrisy, the tribute that vice pays to virtue. They furnished protective coloration, lending an aura of respectability to nefarious practices. Basically, broadcloth was the badge of the gentleman.

The use of "broadcloth" in this sense in combination with "frontier" in the title of this address points toward the pivotal idea around which its thought revolves.

The central idea, then, is that Alexander Campbell was a man who had characteristics of mind and personality that were in contrast with the frontier environment in which he did his pioneering work. But the matter is not quite that simple. He had, in fact, two sets of characteristics, so that the contrast was partly within himself. The world of Alexander Campbell also had contrasts within itself so that his total environment included a wide gamut ranging from the crudities of the American frontier to the cultivated and scholarly circles which formed the background of his very early years and the burgeoning and blossoming American culture which, intermittently at least, provided the setting for his life and work during his middle and later years. If this seems to complicate to the point of confusion what appeared to start out as a simple contrast between a cultured gentleman and a tough neighborhood, it is safer to risk a little confusion than to avoid it by oversimplification of what was not, after all, a very simple situation.

As to Mr. Campbell's qualities of personality, it is, of course, common knowledge to all who know anything at all about him, that he came to be recognized as a cultured gentleman—scholarly, urbane, courteous, and eloquent. He was a man trained in the classics, a student (though not a graduate) at an ancient European university, bookish in his tastes, widely read in history and literature, familiar with the standard books in philosophy and theology, polished (though admittedly redundant) in his literary style and no less polished though perhaps a little ponderous in his manners, sensitive to the amenities of good society, and appreciative of the luxuries of "gracious living" when he became able to afford them. In short, he was a "gentleman" by every standard except that of hereditary wealth—and that standard had no standing on his side of the Atlantic. Yet he was also the bold innovator, leaving the beaten paths of religious thought and ecclesiastical regularity and daring to explore untrodden ways. This he did on a terrain so recently opened and so sparsely settled that it required something of the pioneer's spirit of adventure to live in it at all and more than a modicum of physical stamina and mental fortitude to hold his own in the rough competition of the frontier and come out a respected and "successful" citizen.

The first decade or two of Campbell's life in America were spent in a region in which the society, though not in absolutely the first stage of pioneering, was still crude, simple, and, as seen from our point of view, not far removed from the primitive. The Cane Ridge church in Kentucky, now enclosed in a handsome protecting structure, was a log house of some size and dignity, but the log house is always a relatively primitive form of architecture. The Brush Run church, which the Christian Association of Washington (Pennsylvania) planned, built, and occupied within five weeks after it had decided to become a church, was a timber-framed building, eighteen by thirty-six feet. Its ragged remnants, precious as they are, can scarcely do justice to the original structure. But a church building that could easily be transformed, after it had served during its first seventeen years as the spiritual home of some of the best people in the community, into a blacksmith shop, a village post office, and a stable, is reasonable evidence that the general state of affairs at that time and place was not far removed from that of a frontier. This was the situation into which young Alexander Campbell, a new arrival from the old country and from the University of Glasgow, had to fit himself.

As the religious movement that he initiated gained adherents throughout the Mississippi Valley, he was called upon to make long journeys to the South and West into regions which—in spite of such cultural islands as Lexington and Nashville—were in an even earlier frontier stage than the district of his own residence. He had not merely to appear to be, but actually to be, in congenial contact with the denizens of these regions. It was essential to the performance of his function and the carrying out of his mission to be a pioneer among the pioneers—and he was. This never affected either his manners or his speech, but it did affect his mode of thinking. Or if it did not affect it, then it revealed the harmony that already existed between them.

It would be superfluous to clutter this discussion with detailed evidence that America west of the Alleghenies was in a frontier stage in the early decades of the nineteenth century, or that the newly arrived settlers in that area exhibited both the virtues and the limitations of the pioneer character.

That most of the settlers west of the mountains were newly arrived is evident from the statistics which show an almost incredibly rapid increase of the population. The census of 1800 reported that nine tenths of the country's slightly more than 5,000,000 inhabitants lived east of the Alleghenies, and that more than half of the other tenth were in Kentucky and Tennessee. The entire Northwest Territory—which was to become the populous states of Ohio, Indiana, Illinois, Michigan, and Wisconsin—had only 51,000 inhabitants, and nine tenths of these were in Ohio. (Illinois, Michigan, and Wisconsin had none to speak of.) In the area that was to become these five states, the increase of population in each of the four decades from 1800 to 1840 can be measured not by per cents but by multiples. It was multiplied by five in the first of those decades, by three in the second, was doubled between 1820 and 1830, and redoubled from 1830 to 1840—a cumulative multiplication by 60 in a little more than one generation. By 1840 Ohio ranked third in population among the states of the Union, exceeded only by New York and Pennsylvania, and the latter by only a narrow margin. The fact is that growth of the seaboard states was not merely surpassed by that of the new Western states, it was actually checked by it, for the East was being drained of population by this migration to the West. What happened in the Northwest Territory also happened a little earlier in Kentucky and Tennessee, and a little later and not quite so fast in the Deep South.

This was, therefore, a time when a vast and almost unexplored expanse of raw land was being occupied and subdued, and it took a breed of brawny men and sturdy women to do it. What kind of man, then, was the pioneer?

One immediate and inevitable inference from this rapidity of growth and from the fact that all the communities were new was that the rootage of the pioneer in the particular spot in which he had settled was often relatively tenuous. The urgent thing for him was the solution of his own immediate problems, yet he was generally ready to help his neighbors, if he had any, in doing the jobs that one man could not do alone. All the records give a picture of hospitality and mutual aid on the frontier. It was somewhat later that pride in the community itself developed and when it did, it sometimes reached surprising heights in the beautiful but baseless faith of the citizens of hundreds of hamlets that their town was to become a metropolis.

There was, it must be admitted, a certain amount of truth, if only the truth of caricature, in the derogatory estimate given by the elder Timothy Dwight, president of Yale College from 1795 to 1817, of the pioneers he saw going West in his time.

Always, among the migrants from communities that have attained some measure of culture and stability to the open frontier where everything must be built from the ground up, there is a large element of persons who do not have much to leave behind. Many of these are persons who have fallen out with the older order through economic failure or social maladjustment. The well-established, the satisfied, the conformist, the prosperous and respected do not leave in great numbers the environment to which they are so happily adjusted. Enlarging upon this truism and generalizing upon inadequate observation, Dwight reached the conclusion that the Westward migrants from the seaboard states were, in general, rascals and ne'er-do-wells from whom no good could come. He died too soon to realize how wrong he had been, as proved by the actual course of history.

Of course, the men who made and took the trails to the West, and presently wore those trails into wagon roads, were not the prosperous citizens of Boston and Philadelphia; few of them were graduates of Yale or Harvard, or of King's College which had recently became Columbia, or the College of New Jersey that was later to be rechristened Princeton. Probably the per cent of church members among them, however, would compare favorably with the approximately ten per cent which was about the ratio of church members to total population east of the Alleghenies at the time of the 1800 census; and there is no reason to suppose that the per cent of literacy was less among those who drove the covered wagons than among their former neighbors who had stayed back East.

Basically these pioneers at the time of their migration were people young enough to have most of their lives ahead of them. In any case they had vision enough to sense the boundless opportunities of the mysterious West, and courage and hope enough to take their chances in it. Self-reliance was of the essence of the enterprise. There was little specialization of skills. Everyone must be able to do all the things that most urgently needed to be done.

The pioneer family was very nearly a self-contained unit. It cleared its own land, built its own house, dug its own well, raised (or shot) its own food, spun and wove its own cloth from the wool of its own sheep to make its own clothes and, oftener than not, doctored its own ills with herbs gathered in its own vicinity. The pioneer became magnificently competent in the performance of these simple and primary tasks. The line between producer and consumer was a very short one, for the two were often the same person.

The pioneer's patterns and processes of thought were analogous to the simple, direct and independent procedures which characterized his economic, industrial and social life. He was impatient of intricacies and suspicious of experts. Accustomed to direct action with his own resources in solving the problems and meeting the exigencies of daily life, he was prone to short-cuts in his thinking as in his behavior. As a completely convinced believer in an equalitarian philosophy as applicable to politics, society, and all aspects of human life, he seized avidly on the principle that, since every man was as good as any other man, it must follow that the plain man's common sense was a more trustworthy guide to truth than the opinions of any expert or specialist. There is a suggestive parallel between this characteristic of the frontiersman and one aspect of the almost simultaneous Romantic Movement in Europe, in which praise of the primitive and preference for the unspoiled "child of nature" over the elaborate artificialties of culture and scholarship reached its climax in the "cult of the noble savage" and the description of civilization as "the disease of humanity."[1]

The man of the frontier did not go to that extreme—partly, of course, because he knew the frontier by experience and firsthand, and did not contemplate it through a romantic haze from a comfortable spot in Paris or New York, but partly also,

[1]See Chateaubriand's early work, *Atala,* and James Fenimore Cooper's idealized "Indians."

and even more importantly, because of what he had brought with him into the trackless wilderness. Besides his manly vigor, his self-reliance, and the simplest tools for turning that wilderness into habitable land, he brought the traditions of his race and people. He brought the basic documents of government and religion—the Federal Constitution and the Bible. Among the cultural treasures that were invisible items in his baggage he brought the patterns of social and legal organization. The writ of habeas corpus, the right of trial by jury, the right of representation in legislative assemblies, the general principles of the English common law, the forms of church organization and the basic doctrines of Christianity—these did not have to be invented on the frontier. These were the unseen but indispensable equipment that came along with the tangible baggage on the pack animals and in the Conestoga wagons that cluttered the Westward trails. This is very important. It provided the connecting link between the accumulated values of European, and then of colonial, culture and the new communities that were to spring up on virgin soil. The soil may have been virgin, but the minds of its new occupants had been fertilized by inherited ideas that were the seed of a new culture which was to produce a rich harvest in the new land. The rightful emphasis upon the importance of the frontier in American history has sometimes obscured the dependence of the frontier on its intellectual and cultural base of supplies back East and overseas. It must be noted, too, that the lines of communication with that base of supplies were kept open, and that there was a continuous flow of ideas and of cultural resources along with the flow of population that produced the wonderful increase in population of which we have spoken. One of the truest things that can be said of the American frontier is that there was never anything static about it.

The country immediately began to grow up behind that advancing line of the frontier. An essential fact about mid-America in the first half of the nineteenth century—or, say, from 1809 to

1860, the half century of Alexander Campbell's activity—was its rapid emergence from the frontier conditions to the more developed type of culture which normally appears behind the line of the frontier as it moves Westward. What yesterday was an unmapped wilderness penetrated only by the blazed trails of explorers becomes today a region occupied by many settlers and tomorrow an area dotted with towns and boasting schools and churches. Colleges began to be founded in the midlands in the '30's and '40's, not to mention Transylvania at Lexington which started as a seminary in 1780 and became a "university" in 1800. Some of these colleges lived to become substantial and excellent. Most of them died in infancy, though not without giving an intellectual lift to their communities and constituencies and exercising a beneficent influence that lasted much longer than they did; and most of them were pretty feeble, academically as well as financially. But colleges of any kind are not founded by men in the buckskin-breeches-and-coonskin-cap stage of pioneering. Of all the facts about the frontier, the one most easily overlooked by those who exploit the romantic crudity of the pioneers, along of course with their heroic fortitude and self-reliant individualism, is the fact that these picturesquely primitive conditions never continued very long in any one place. Further, whether on the cutting edge of the frontier or behind it, the cultural pattern was always spotty. There were concentrations of more-advanced culture in some places, and enclaves of almost unmodified primitivism in others, and there were all the shades between.

This was the kind of diversified and changing environment in which our hero lived and did his work. He could do it as successfully as he did because he himself had the two kinds of contrasting qualities. This was the reason he could make such an impact on the society of his time. He could speak to the condition of all its levels because he had all these levels within his own personality.

The pioneer was undoubtedly a man of independence in action and thought, but there were limits to his self-reliance. In his more serious moods he felt the need of some established and authoritative certainties on which to base his independent reasoning and action. As a patriotic American he had the Constitution as the fundamental law, the bedrock of civil institutions and the unquestionable norm of political truth and righteousness. It was not for him to question whether the Constitution was right or not. It *was* right. The only questions were: What does it mean? How does it apply to this or that particular issue? It is a remarkable fact that, after the Bill of Rights and two other amendments (one to give greater security to states' rights and the other to alter an impractical method of electing the President and Vice-President), there was not another amendment to the Constitution during the 61 years from 1804 to 1865.

As the Constitution was the fundamental and infallible authority in the political field, so the Bible was solid bedrock in religion for those who professed to have any religion. It was not for one to question whether the Bible was right or not on any particular matter of doctrine or history. It *was* right. The only legitimate question was, What does it mean? What answers does it give to the questions raised? The individual could assert his right to an authentic judgment on these matters and—still exercising the pioneer's confidence in the competence of the common man's common sense—could claim that his judgment was as good as anybody's; but in general he did not challenge the authority of the documents he interpreted.

On the political side, then, he was a loyal and patriotic American, yet an independent voter, forming his own opinions but liable to be swayed by the persuasions of an eloquent office seeker or the propagandist of a policy who grounded his argument on the certainties of the Constitution. On the religious side, if he were a religious man or were open to the religious appeal, he was a devotee of an authoritarian religion or a prospective convert to one, but free to decide for himself what were the demands of the authority and (just as in politics) susceptible to the blandishments of oratory and to either emotional or argumentative appeal.

There have been few periods in history in which the people in general had such a solid body of common presuppositions as the basis of their thinking and also such a feeling of their own freedom and competence in making their own decisions as to specific beliefs and practices. This was the American frontier considered as a state of mind, not as a geographical area. This was the pioneering characteristic that had most effect in both religion and politics and that lasted longest—even down to our own times—as the controlling pattern in the thinking of a great segment of the American people and as an important, if not dominant, factor for most of them.

It is in these respects that Alexander Campbell was a pioneer in his thinking and for this reason that he could speak to the understanding and to the hearts of his constituency. He was also a pioneer in the sense that he broke some new ground and made some bold innovations in religious thought. At one level of his thinking his attitudes, his presuppositions and his mental processes were those of the frontier people whom he addressed. He spoke a more urbane language, embellished his utterances with flowers of rhetoric culled from the garden of English literature, and presented himself to them as what must have seemed to them, and really was, a figure of dignity, polish, and culture which they could admire but could seldom emulate. But the fundamental structure of his thinking was theirs. Like them, he had an immutable and unquestionable basis of certainty in the words of Holy Writ—even though he had also some "rules of interpretation" that were new to them and which anticipated the critical processes which he followed only a step or two. He appealed to the common sense of the unlearned and regarded the ordinary man as sufficiently competent to make his own interpretations in the matters which most vitally affected his eternal welfare and the structure and operations of the church. He could brush off the theological experts, assert the irrelevance of their scholastic subleties, and invite the plain man to use his own good sense in interpreting the infallible words of Holy Writ. He could refer to the biblical writers as the "inspired amanuenses," with the implication that all they had had to do was to write down on parchment the words that the Holy Spirit whispered in their ears. He may or may not have known that Luther before him had declared that "The Holy Spirit is the all-simplest writer" and that therefore anyone who could read at all could understand the one exact meaning of the sacred text if his mind was open and his heart was right. Whether he did or not, his approach to this attitude was by a different route. For Luther it was a rejection of the "Catholic tradition" as the norm of interpretation, and of the multiple meanings—historical, allegorical, analogical and anagogical, and cabalistic which had more recently been exploited by Reuchlin and others. For Campbell it was an escape from the Protestant scholasticism which had confined the right of interpretation to the theologians and had crystallized their findings in authoritative creeds, and an affirmation of the principle, dear to the mind of the frontier, that "the wayfaring man, though a fool, need not err therein."

This was an application of the principle of democracy in the field of religion. How quickly this young Irishman became Americanized. How congenial to his mind was the spirit of the new country to which he so promptly yielded his admiration and his loyalty. He came to it as though it were that toward which he had been groping. When he found it, he knew that he was at home, though the salt spray was still in his hair. He quickly assumed the leadership of the movement his father was in the act of initiating. His was the more plastic as well as the more dynamic personality.

We must not claim too much novelty and uniqueness for the frontier principle of insistence on the liberty and competence of the individual in the realm of spiritual truth for two reasons:

First, there have always been bold spirits, and sometimes whole groups of them, who resisted the standardized orthodoxies of their time and practiced this principle of the frontier, even when they did not affirm it. Some of them became martyrs to their courage. Some, like the mystics of the Middle Ages, skirted the brink of heresy without falling under the church's ban. (The very word "heresy" means "one's own opinion," as contrasted with an opinion that has been signed, sealed, and certified by the constituted authorities.) Every radical reformer is a rebel, and every rebel rests his case ultimately on the individual's right to hold his own opinion. Left-wing Puritanism in seventeenth-century England was a seething complex of such radical individualists. John Milton was a shining light as a gentleman adventurer in fields of thought beyond the respectable authorized doctrines of his day. The American heritage from these rebellious groups was an invaluable element in the formation of the American tradition of civil rights and religious liberty. Perhaps never elsewhere or earlier had there been a whole social order in which the voice of authority was so weak, the spirit of individualism so strong, and the freedom of the individual so generally affirmed as a matter of principle, as on the American frontier.

Second, even on the frontier there was that inevitable tendency for rebels to set limits to their own rebellion, to establish new authorities or revive old ones, to set up new authoritative norms and structures which might become as rigid as those against which they had rebelled. The American "denominational system" is a perfect illustration of this process: first, the attainment of liberty to dissent, as against any restraint by the police power of a state doing the bidding and protecting the interests of an established church; then, the exercise of the right of the like-minded to organize their own groups; and finally, the building of walls and closing the gates of these groups to exclude all who did not conform to their respective bodies of practice and opinion.

Yet there remained an unprecedented degree of fluidity in the total situation, for two reasons: first, because those who could not or would not conform to the requirement of any of these groups had the civil right to withdraw or to remain outside and to form groups of their own if they wished; and second, because such a large majority of the population, though having a decent respect for Christianity in a general way, had no specific commitment to it and were members of no church. Those who were out could stay out if they chose. Those who were in had come in of their own free will and could get out if the requirements of their denominations became irksome to them. So the principle of individualism triumphed after all.

This was the scene upon which Alexander Campbell entered and in which he did his work. I am calling him a pioneer because he fitted so perfectly into the environment which I have been describing. Thomas Campbell, in his great pronunciamento, the "Declaration and Address," had stressed the fact that America was a uniquely favorable place for the great experiment he proposed to initiate. Alexander Campbell subscribed to every word that his father had written and proceeded to demonstrate the correctness of his estimate. It *was* a uniquely favorable place, and his own temperament and convictions, as well as his father's, were admirably fitted to work under these conditions. Their whole proposal was predicated on the presupposition that the great bodies of theology embodied in the creeds of the denominations were not "revealed truth" but were compilations of "human opinions" and that every man has the right to form his own opinions. Practically all Americans agreed that men had that legal right as against any restraint or compulsion by the state. The Campbells declared that this was also a Christian right as against the demand of any church for conformity to its creed. Therefore a united church could embrace within its generous bosom the holders of the widest possible diversity of theological opinions. This was indeed the very gist of their proposal for the union of Christians in One Church.

Even when Mr. Campbell had developed a theology of his own he did not wish to make the acceptance of it a condition of fellowship with the movement he was leading. When he published his *Christian System,* his critics shouted with glee that, after all his denunciation of creeds, Alexander Campbell had at last broken down and written a creed for his church. They were wrong. It was never intended as a creed, and it was never used as a creed.

And, after all, the most important and significant point about Alexander Campbell's theology was the use he made of it. It was not a creed. It was not claimed to be a statement of all truth. It was not the theology of a church. It was simply *Alexander Campbell's* theology.[2]

Mr. Campbell never canonized his own writings or erected his beliefs into a standard of orthodoxy for his associates and followers; yet there developed a tendency among many influential leaders of the movement to do something very much like that. While they were taking so much pride in categorizing the great dogmatic declaration of the historic creeds as matters of "human opinion" in regard to which Christians had liberty and upon which therefore there was no reason for division, other issues were brought forward upon which they could be as dogmatic as the majority at Nicaea was on *homoousion* and the

[2]Closing paragraph of *Alexander Campbell's Theology,* by Winfred E. Garrison, Christian Publishing Co., St. Louis, 1900.

"procession of the Holy Ghost," or Calvin on predestination. This ambiguity of attitude can be viewed as the resultant of a mingling of frontier simplicities and independence with a historic tradition brought over from the whole stream of Christian thought. Mr. Campbell himself shared in this ambiguity.

The broadcloth aspect of Alexander Campbell's mind and personality—his appropriation of the intellectual and spiritual heritage of the Christian centuries before him, his sophistication, in the good sense—leaps to the eye of any reader of the record of his life and work. He moved with grace and dignity among the great of his time. On his preaching and lecturing tours to the Eastern cities and to the cultural centers of the South, he was as much at home as he was on the expanding acres of his farm. When he went down to Richmond to take his place in that famous Virginia Constitutional Convention of 1829, it did not take long for his fellow members to learn that he was a man to be reckoned with in debate. Reading some of those debates in which he crossed logical and rhetorical swords with John Marshall and John Randolph gives one a tingling of the spine even now and leaves the impression that, though the Eastern slave-owning element in the convention outvoted him, he had the better of it in argument and eloquence.

Campbell's first two debates got a good deal of subsequent publicity through their publication, but the debates themselves were with little-known men at little-known country towns. His third and fourth were in Cincinnati—one with a Roman Catholic Archbishop, the other with an internationally famous socialist, social reformer, and opponent of all religions. The fifth was in Lexington, with one of the ablest Presbyterian theologians of his generation as his opponent and with Henry Clay as "president of the board of moderators."

Things like these give a clear enough indication that the man was equipped, by education and experience added to natural endowments, to deal at least on even terms with the best that America had to offer in the upper levels of its culture. What is more significant for our purpose is that these manifestations of gentility were not superficial but rested on a pretty solid foundation of learning and a very considerable capacity for original creative thinking. The studious atmosphere in which he had been reared and his own intellectual diligence compensated for the limitation of his university work to one academic year—actually only from November to the following May. He was well read in history and literature and in the more important theological works that were current in his earlier years. Under his father's direction he had thoroughly absorbed the philosophy of John Locke—whom he calls "the Christian philosopher"—and he knew the devastating results of its non-Christian developments both in England and France. Except for this, and probably a direct or indirect acquaintance with Thomas Reid's "Common Sense philosophy," which was the pride of Glasgow University in his time, he probably did not know much about philosophy. Coleridge had imported some aspects of German philosophy into England, but Campbell considered him too vague and foggy to be of much value. Kant and the early post-Kantians certainly made no impact on his mind. The English utilitarians, Bentham and Mill, were too nearly his contemporaries to get much attention from one who soon got too busy with practical affairs and urgent issues to keep abreast of philosophical developments that did not have an obvious bearing on religion.

Of greater importance in any picture of Campbell's mind is his realization that, as an interpreter of Christianity and a reformer of the church, he was building on foundations that had been laid by earlier Christian thinkers. His extensive reading in church history saved him from the illusion, shared by many untutored reformers and by many of his own followers, that nothing of any importance had happened between the end of the Apostolic Age and the dawning light of the particular reformation they were promoting. When a critic attempted to belittle his contribution on some point by saying that he had "borrowed" from an earlier writer, Campbell replied that he had borrowed (if you want to call it that) many things from many sources and that he would be poor indeed if he were deprived of all he had inherited from the mighty spirits of all the Christian centuries. Such recognition of his place within, not above, the stream of Christian thought is one of the marks of the sanity and maturity of Mr. Campbell's mind.

In his attitude toward the Bible and in his use of it, he showed a mingling of not wholly consistent qualities. On the one hand were the famous "Rules of Interpretation," as laid down in his *Christian System*. He held that to find the meaning and application of any passage and its relevance to the duty of Christian men, one must ask: Who wrote it, and when, and to whom, and in what connection? The initial suggestion for this no doubt came from the Covenant Theology which had stressed the distinction between the successive covenants, or dispensations, in the history of God's dealings with men. Campbell's actual use of this principle was to draw a sharp line between the Hebrew dispensation and the Christian—so sharp, indeed, that he was sometimes accused, quite unjustly, of "throwing away the Old Testament." But the recognition of this distinction led him on logically to insistence on giving consideration to the authorship, time, place, purpose, and circumstances of any passage of Holy Writ that might be cited for doctrine or instruction. One might think he was writing a prospectus for biblical study by the methods of Higher Criticism. He never went that far, but he did go far enough to free himself forever from the temptation to clinch any argument by an undiscriminating declaration that "the Bible says." In this he was far from the rustic simplicity of the frontier and also far ahead of the insights of his orthodox scholarly contemporaries.

Yet there was also in Campbell's thinking a strain of pioneer primitivism. It took the form of oversimplification of problems that are not simple and a preference for rural plainness over any kind or degree of urban elegance in everything related to the church. He wrote scornfully of "great cathedrals costing forty thousand dollars." His view of "primitive Christianity" was that it should *look* primitive as well as *be* primitive in the essentials of its faith and practice. He oversimplified the matter of divine revelation and the inspiration of Scripture—but then nearly all Christian theologians before his time had done that. The biblical writers were the "inspired amanuenses," and God had used words "in their ordinary and accepted sense" in dictating his communications to them.

It was Thomas Campbell's statement that "the New Testament is as perfect a constitution for the worship, discipline, and government of the New Testament church, and as perfect a rule for the particular duties of its members, as the Old Testament was for the worship, discipline, and government of the Old Testament church and the particular duties of its members" (Proposition 4 in the "Address"). But Alexander Campbell accepted this and made it the basis of the details of his program. On this presupposition, he worked out "a particular ecclesiastical order" (Walter Scott's phrase) which he regarded as the one and only form that a pure church could have. The proposal to "restore primitive Christianity," in the sense of restoring a complete program of worship, discipline, government, and faith so clearly and authoritatively exhibited in the New Testament that no element of "human opinion" need enter into it, was not only primitive but naïve to the last degree. Here was the frontier's habit of oversimplification in an extreme form. The proposition seemed plausible at the time. But as social conditions became more complex and as the church's responsibilities in the fields of evangelism, missions, and education were most fully realized, controversies and divisions arose about the means that could be legitimately adopted in the performance of these functions. The slogan "restoration of primitive Christianity" had so much real value in it, considered as a summons to eliminate the doctrines and dogmas of later coinage from the conditions of Christian fellowship, that it could not easily be given up; but the use of it as providing divine sanction for some specific pattern of procedure covering all the church's activities and operations tended to nullify the appeal for unity which it had been designed to promote. Mr. Campbell himself gradually grew away from such literalistic use of the slogan, but not soon enough or far enough to save his followers from the confusions and divisions which it engendered.

An estimate of Alexander Campbell should not end on this negative note. True, a part of his mind was dominated by narrow, rigid and literalistic views which, if not derived from the conditions of pioneer life in a new country, are certainly congenial to the mentality of those who live on the undeveloped frontiers of culture. The other kind of pioneer characteristics, however, was much more prominent in his character—the courage to explore new territory and attempt new enterprises; the independence to challenge old opinions and make his own search for truth; the fortitude to endure for a lifetime through dangers and difficulties and against whatever opposition might arise until he had reached, not indeed the pinnacle of his aim, for no true pioneer ever does that, but a substantial plateau of achievement. If to have these qualities together with the limitations that normally go with them is to be a pioneer, then Alexander Campbell was a pioneer. If broadcloth can be taken as the symbol of a gentleman, and if "gentleman" can be generously interpreted to mean a man who has appropriated and assimilated his full share of the cultural heritage of the race, has oriented himself in the stream of history and in the best in the society of his own time, and is equipped to give copiously and graciously as he has received abundantly, then he was a "Pioneer in Broadcloth."

The Drama of Alexander Campbell

LOUIS COCHRAN

Lawyer, novelist, and author of **The Fool of God**

When I first became interested in the possibilities of a novel on the life of Alexander Campbell, I was warned by most of my friends, a few of whom considered themselves authorities in church history, that I was wasting my time. However admirable Campbell might be as a religious leader, educator, and apostle of Christian unity, he was, they said, uninteresting, even dull as a *person;* that rare type of individual whose intellect always ruled his heart; a man of prodigious learning and labors, but a man in whom a cold sense of duty and moral perfection overrode all other considerations. Such people may be paragons of the highest virtue, great reformers, and leaders of enduring movements for the betterment of mankind, but they inspire little affection in even the warmest human heart.

There was no human drama in the life of Alexander Campbell, so I was told; no elements of real personal risk, or sacrifice; no uncertain tortuous struggles, no mighty conflicts. He was a man set apart from his fellows by many fortuitous gifts, including the acquisition by marriage of a fine farm, and he knew it. As a warm, personable human being, with faults and foibles as well as virtues, he was a total loss. There were no deeds of derring-do, no passionate decisions, no costs uncounted for love or righteousness' sake. His personal life, insofar as human interest was concerned, was as dull as dishwater, and except as an exercise in theology or church history, any effort to write a book on him would be love's labor lost.

But, in the final analysis, the pessimists were wrong, as pessimists always are.

Alexander Campbell was more than the leader of a world movement to restore New Testament Christianity through the elimination of human creeds; more than the founder of Bethany College; more than the editor-publisher of that inspiring, sometimes caustic and iconoclastic religious magazine, *The Christian Baptist,* and the wiser and more tolerant *Millennial Harbinger,* both of which had world-wide circulation and still influence religious thought. Alexander Campbell was more, much more, than a devoted husband, and the proud father of fourteen children; more than a statesman and a foremost private citizen of his adopted country, known far and wide during his later years by the unacknowledged title of "the Bishop," and "the Sage of Bethany." He was more a public figure whose human characteristics have been too much obscured not only by his enemies—and he had bitter enemies—but by his followers who in their writings and disputations over his theological doctrines have almost completely overlooked the colorful, drama-packed episodes of his long life, as well as the human blemishes which identify him with us as an imperfect member of the human race and therefore kin to the Adam within us all.

In any analysis, Alexander Campbell was a tremendous human being; a great champion of human freedom and religious liberty, and the foremost advocate in modern times of Christian unity.

In his prime Campbell was as distinguished-looking a Virginia gentleman as one would hope to find even in Richmond. His most familiar likeness, the portrait painted in his forty-ninth year by Bogle, reveals a clean-shaven, dignified man with deep-set, blue eyes under dark, bushy eyebrows, topped by a flowing mane of white hair over a high, broad forehead; wide, firm chin cupped in a white stock and cravat set off by the black broadcloth which was the traditional hallmark of the clergyman of that period. He was not, we are told, a particularly handsome man. His features were irregular; his nose too long and slightly hooked, tilted noticeably to the right; his face too stern for easy familiarity.

He was not an unusually tall man, or big physically in any way, although such was the force of his personality, his brilliant mind, and his deep convictions that he created the effect of unusual stature and power. Throughout his long life wherever Alexander Campbell sat was the head of the table. He was actually five feet eleven inches in height, with an average weight of about 175 pounds; his shoulders were broad but slightly inclined in the "scholar's stoop"; he was long-legged and long-armed, and during middle life he had the beginnings of a paunch. His voice was neither deep nor full, but high, clear, and penetrating, with a resonant quality that enabled him to be easily heard in any assembly; his manner of public speaking differed sharply from that of most preachers of that period. Abraham Lincoln once said that when he went to preaching, he wanted his preacher to show some action as if he were fighting a swarm of bees—a standard too much adhered to by speakers of that day. Lincoln was twenty-one years younger than Campbell and, so far as the record shows, never heard him preach but, if he had, he would have heard a speaker who ignored the bees, and yet held his audience captive through two- and three-hour sermons. It is said Mr. Campbell rarely raised his voice. Standing beside the pulpit or upon the rostrum, leaning slightly forward, often upon his cane, his thoughts flowed in a smooth, cascading stream of words so that his listeners sometimes unconsciously rose in their seats and leaned forward, fearful lest they miss some of the riches of Christian wisdom as his mind unlocked its storehouse and poured out the treasures he had accumulated there during the years.

Alexander Campbell was always in a hurry; the days were too short, the years never long enough for all he hoped to accomplish. When he walked, he walked rapidly. Sometimes his steps were irregular as though he was unable to make up his mind whether to walk or run; when he rode on horseback, he rode stooped slightly forward as if to hasten the movement of his mount. When he shook hands, there was no lingering over the handclasp, no polite, perfunctory conversation. He lived many lives in one: he was a religious reformer in the great succession of Luther and Knox, Calvin and Wesley, publisher, preacher, reformer, statesman, editor, educator, farmer, and businessman as well as patriarch to a swarming host of relatives and relatives-in-law. The world called him eminent in all his lines.

There is high drama in the fact that he made good his resolve as a penniless youth to preach the unity of God's people at his own expense; that he would accept no pay for his preaching.

"Then, my son," his father warned him, "you will wear many a ragged coat!"

However, he wore no ragged coats, unless by choice, and at no time did he personally accept any financial remuneration for his preaching although he was often a beggar for Bethany College. During his earlier years he had some remarks to make about the "hireling, stall-fed clergy," who, he said, were too much concerned with their salaries, and openly advocated that they should do as he did, make their living by secular pursuits and preach only for the glory of the Lord. One of the reasons Alexander Campbell was both a very human man and a great one was that though he made mistakes, he had the capacity to grow in wisdom and the courage to change his mind. In his riper years he came to see that every laborer is worthy of his hire, and advocated a reasonable compensation for the preachers, few of whom would be fortunate enough to marry daughters of wealthy farmers or possess his business abilities. But the mischief had been done. For many years the Restoration Movement was plagued by preachers who were small farmers, or blacksmiths, or merchants, or what-have-you, by vocation, and preachers of the gospel as the urge led them, citing as their exemplar and apostle the great Alexander Campbell himself.

Alexander Campbell was the exception to the general rule. From the time of his marriage to Margaret Brown at the age of twenty-two until his death at seventy-eight, he was not only a religious reformer of growing power and influence but one of the most successful businessmen of his day. He acquired land and more land, nurturing it with the wisdom and affection of a true lover of the soil. He became one of the earliest sheep owners in his area, breeding fine herds of Merino sheep. He found time to preside at interstate conventions of wool growers from Steubenville to Springfield, Massachusetts. He was, also, for over forty years a foremost editor and publisher. The Lord, indeed, marvelously blessed this penniless Scotch-Irish immigrant boy of 1809 in all his undertakings, and when fifty-seven years later he went to his eternal reward, he not only had paid his own way throughout a long ministry but he left behind him an estate valued by his executors at approximately $200,000, one of the wealthiest at that time in Virginia.

If the Lord blessed him in his business enterprises, it was surely not merely to confound his enemies. Without the financial independence of Alexander Campbell and his resultant ability for fifty years to preach the gospel of apostolic Christianity without interference, there probably would have been no reformation, or Restoration Movement, no Disciples of Christ, Christian Church, or Church of Christ, as we speak of them today, and no Bethany College. The cause of Christian unity based upon the Holy Scriptures alone might yet be waiting for a world spokesman. The biblical injunction to "seek first his kingdom and his righteousness, and all these things shall be yours as well" has never been more dramatically demonstrated than in the life of Alexander Campbell. His ability to accumulate a fortune was the least important and dramatic aspect in his life.

All his life Alexander Campbell stood apart from partisan politics but in 1829 he permitted his name to be placed before the voters as a delegate to the nonpolitical, nonpartisan Virginia Constitutional Convention.

"What business had I in such matters?" he wrote his friend, William Tener of Londonderry, in 1830. "I will tell you. I consented to be elected because, first, I was desirous of laying a foundation for the abolition of slavery. . . ."

The method he advocated for the elimination of this evil was to fix upon a day which by constitutional provision would be the last day any person could be born a slave in the state of Virginia. But his method was not adopted.

The Virginia Constitutional Convention which convened at Richmond in October, 1829, included some of the most distinguished citizens of the country, among them two former Presidents, James Monroe and James Madison; a future President, John Tyler; and Chief Justice John Marshall. The young delegate from Brooke County was the only member of the Convention who was an ordained minister. At first, because of his clerical calling, and possibly because he preached every night during the three-month session in various pulpits of the community, his fellow delegates looked askance upon him. But long before the Convention adjourned the following January, he had made his place secure as one of the ablest and most respected public servants among them, though he was to fail in his dream of the abolition of slavery and his other principal reforms. However, time eventually caught up with him, and, in a sense, he won his greatest battle. Part of the drama of this extraordinary man of God is that the almost half-million Christians who looked upon him as their leader in the Restoration Movement did *not* divide into sectional factions with the later catastrophe of the Civil War as did so many church parties. In both the North and the South, they remained firmly united in the primitive faith of the New Testament Church, holding within their hearts that passion for unity, that leaven that is stirring the Christian world today, demonstrating before all history that it *can* be done; that God's people can stand united even amidst the horrors and hatreds of a fratricidal war.

There is an epic quality in the drama of Alexander Campbell as a boy of eighteen stepping into his father's shoes when Thomas Campbell sailed for America in April, 1807, and leading his mother and six younger children through storm and shipwreck and a winter's stay in a strange land before crossing the Atlantic Ocean to join their preacher-father in the New World. The wreck of the *Hibernia,* in which they first set sail, off the Scottish coast; Alexander's dedication to a life of Christian service; his salvage of his father's books before he would take the last boat for shore; the providential year at the University of Glasgow where his father had graduated twenty-five years before; and their subsequent safe arrival in New York harbor, is one of those inspiring our faith that man is invincible and immortal and may be truly led of God.

We must not overlook the drama of Alexander's rejection, while still a student at Glasgow, of the leaden token, symbol of sectarian exclusiveness and religious bigotry of the Anti-Burgher Branch of the Associate, or Seceder, Church of Scotland. This token would have permitted him to participate in the ceremony of the Lord's Supper, to the exclusion of other Christians who did not believe precisely as did he. There was drama in the meeting of Alexander and Thomas Campbell after a separation of almost three years when they discovered that, though thousands of miles apart and without any communication on the subject, they had both reached the conclusion that all those who accept Jesus Christ and follow his teachings to the best of their knowledge and ability are entitled to partake of the Sacrament of the Lord's Supper, and to be accepted by all other followers of Christ as fellow Christians.

Through such episodes in his early life as the Buffalo Seminary, the boarding school for boys which he operated for five years in his home; *The Christian Baptist*, the journal of religious opinion which was to establish him as one of the world's great religious thinkers; his dissatisfaction and eventual break with the Baptist denomination in which he and his father, Thomas, had taken refuge; his futile efforts to bring the National Road near Bethany in order to make that community more accessible to the outside world—through all these we see the beginnings of that fascinating drama of conflict with other religious leaders, with powerful national interests, and with himself which was to characterize Alexander Campbell all his life. Who among the students of church history has not read and chuckled over the inadequacies of human creeds so vividly portrayed in *The Christian Baptist* in that inimitable "Parable of the Iron Bedstead"? His parody of the 13th chapter of the Acts of the Apostles, the setting aside of Paul and Barnabas as missionaries to the Gentiles, is devastating in its exposure of the weaknesses of human vanity; his strictures on "complimentary prayers," or "prayers addressed to human beings not yet deified," once so common in our pulpits, and that brilliant satire, "The Third Epistle of Peter," subtitled "A Looking Glass for the Clergy," will become obsolete only when the church can say it is at last without fault.

Indeed, *The Christian Baptist* contains some of the wisest and most tolerant of Christian writings. In his May, 1826, "Letter to an Independent Baptist" who had protested his association with other religious parties, Alexander Campbell revealed himself to be as all-inclusive and as modern as tomorrow's sunrise in his statement on tolerance and understanding among Christians.

"This plan of making our own nest, and fluttering over our own brood; of building our own tent, and of confining all goodness and grace to our noble selves and the 'elect few' who are like us, is the quintessence," he said, "of sublimated pharisaism."

Eleven years later there appeared in the *Millennial Harbinger,* that wise successor to the *Christian Baptist,* his immortal definition of a Christian given in his reply to an unnamed lady of Lunenburg, Virginia, who had taken him to task for daring to say that he found Christian believers in all religious parties.

"Who is a Christian?" he asked. "I answer, Every one that believes in his heart that Jesus of Nazareth is the Messiah, the Son of God; repents of his sins, and obeys him in all things according to his measure of knowledge of his will."

In 1827 he published the first modern-speech version of the New Testament, calling it in later editions *The Living Oracles,* and causing John Randolph of Roanoke, considered the most caustic wit in America, to shake his fist at Campbell during a debate in the Virginian Constitutional Convention, and to declare in baffled exasperation: "That man is never satisfied! God Almighty could not satisfy him with the Bible which He gave the world, and Mr. Campbell had to go and write a new one of his own!"

To a degree, Mr. Randolph was correct. Throughout his long life, Alexander Campbell was never satisfied with anything less than the whole truth—an uncompromising, unyielding protagonist on the stage of human history for the right as he saw it.

No role he played was more exciting, or perhaps more rewarding, than that of the founder of Bethany College, "the only College known to us in the civilized world founded upon the Bible," as he wrote in the *Millennial Harbinger*. At the age of fifty-two, when most men are beginning to seek shelter for their declining years, Alexander Campbell created and shouldered new burdens which alone could have crushed many a younger man. But though he had no organization or endowment behind him, he had a national reputation as a religious leader, an infinite trust in God, his own private fortune, and no false modesty in seeking funds from his friends. He donated the land for the campus, assumed the responsibility for the erection and equipment of the first buildings, and served as teacher, counselor, President, dominant influence, and chief money-raiser of the College until his death in 1866.

The drama inherent in the spectacle of two dynamic religious movements merging into an onrushing element of history is seen in the meeting of Alexander Campbell and Barton W. Stone at Georgetown, Kentucky, in 1824. Stone was then fifty-two years old, once a Presbyterian but for almost a quarter of a century groping his way out of the jungle of human creeds and dogma, his followers, some 15,000 of them in the South and West, designating themselves as "Christians only." Campbell was thirty-six, also once a Presbyterian but since 1813 a member, if somewhat precariously, of the Baptists, though he was called a "reforming Baptist." The older man was like Thomas Campbell, gentle and conciliatory; the younger, bold, aggressive, with a rationalistic approach to the problems of Christian unity as contrasted with the more emotional approach of Stone. But despite their differences, there was no disparity in their common devotion to the New Testament teachings, and the unity of the Church of Christ. As Stone later said, "Our views were one."

They met again during Campbell's Kentucky tour of 1830, and in January, 1832, at Lexington, Kentucky, there began the union of their two religious groups, the "Reformed Baptists" of Alexander Campbell and the "Christians" of Barton W. Stone. Campbell was not present at this first union, which was between Kentuckians. Indeed, he was inclined to be a little skeptical of it, since there were many minor issues to be settled, but soon he bent all his efforts to its support. They both preached and practiced that fundamental rule, first proclaimed by Thomas Campbell, "Where the Scriptures speak, we speak; where the Scriptures are silent, we are silent" and the classic maxim coined long before by Rupertus Meldenius, "In essentials, unity; in nonessentials, liberty; in all things, charity." But though most of their minor differences, the nonessentials, were in due time resolved, there was one difference. The choice of a name, whether to be called "Christians," as Stone preferred, or "Disciples," as recommended by Campbell, was unresolved and has remained to plague us unto this day.

There is always high drama in the spectacle of men's minds in conflict, and the debates of Alexander Campbell rank unsurpassed in the religious field, equalled in forensic power and brilliance only by the Webster-Hayne and the Lincoln-Douglas debates in the political arena. Campbell agreed to his first public debate reluctantly, after having twice refused. Only after much persuasion by his then fellow Baptists did he accept the challenge of John Walker, a Presbyterian minister, who doubted the efficacy or inspiration of baptism by immersion. Three years later he engaged in another debate, again on baptism and again with a Presbyterian, W. D. Maccalla. The third of his debates, and possibly the most dramatic, was with the world-famous capitalist-reformer-atheist, Robert Owen of New Lanark, whose activities at that time included the operation of a socialist, atheistic colony at New Harmony, Indiana. Owen apparently sincerely believed that society could be redeemed if the "evils of private property, marriage, and religion could be eliminated," although he made no move to rid himself of his own considerable fortune, and throughout a long life cherished his own happy marriage to a wife who never forsook her religious faith.

The debate with Owen was held at the Old Stone Church of the Methodists on East Fifth Street in Cincinnati in April, 1829, and attracted wide attention. For Alexander Campbell it was one of the significant milestones of his life. Incredible as it may seem today, there were many at that time who regarded him as an evil genius whose purpose it was to wreck organized religion, but now that he stood before the world as the champion of Christianity against the foremost atheist of his day, it could no longer be said of him that he was the devil's hatchet man. Alexander Campbell and his followers had at last become respectable.

As he was the champion of Christianity against atheism, so also was he the champion of all Protestantism when in January, 1837, he debated Catholic Bishop John B. Purcell on the Bishop's statement that "the Protestant Reformation has been the cause of all the contention and infidelity in the world." If this may be considered today, even by Catholics, as an extravagant statement, so also may be the thesis of the eloquent retort delivered by Mr. Campbell that the Catholic Church was "the 'Babylon' of John, the 'Man of sin' of Paul, and the Empire of the 'Youngest Horn' of Daniel's Sea Monster." But this debate was not all extravaganza. Far from it! The week's discussion, held in the Sycamore Street Christian Church of Cincinnati, summarized and analyzed the entire range of the differences between Protestantism and Roman Catholicism, and is one of the finest expositions of their fundamental beliefs and differences ever given. It is also the last time in recorded church history that a Catholic bishop and a Protestant clergyman debated their religious differences in public.

The fifth, the last, the longest, and in some respects the most important of Campbell's debates was held in Lexington, Kentucky, in 1843 with Dr. Nathan L. Rice, a Presbyterian minister. Henry Clay was the chief moderator. To some extent this sixteen-day debate was simply a controversy between the theology of Dr. Rice and that of Mr. Campbell, but it was also one of the most complete and authoritative discussions of the arguments for and against human religious creeds ever held, and as such is read and recognized today.

Alexander Campbell has sometimes been accused of being unnecessarily caustic in his references to those of different religious persuasion, particularly during his younger days, but in that respect he was but the child of his times. Those were the days of personal attack in print, and on public platforms, and in person, between advocates of different faiths, and Campbell's language, even in the most violent days of *The Christian Baptist,* was mild and inoffensive when compared to that of his enemies. But this forbearance did not save him from the most savage attack. Alexander Campbell was hailed into court three times on charges of libel; twice being actually arrested, and on the last occasion spent a week in a Glasgow prison before the warrant for his arrest was dismissed by the superior court as illegal. That each of his complainants was also a minister of the gospel, and that none of the suits ever came to trial, proves nothing except the intensity of the opposition he aroused, and the personal nature of the religious controversy of the times.

If he was deeply suspect as "a beloved missionary of the devil," as one religious periodical characterized him, he was, also, despite his reputation for cold intellectuality, much loved by those who knew him best. And he was, personally, a man of deep though reserved and wholly unselfish affection, as revealed by his close family life and his complete devotion to his friends.

His gifts were many; he was also a man of many sorrows. Death was a frequent and a lingering guest in his home. Part of the drama and the greatness of Alexander Campbell was his ability to rise above personal grief and misfortune, as well as success, and never to surrender in Christian hope. The Alexander Campbell who so early buried the wife of his youth and ten of his children, and who in his seventieth year, an old man failing in health, helplessly watched the college of his dreams almost disappear in flames, and then set forth without complaint to build again from its ashes, was a man of inspired vision and courage whose stature before the world grows with each passing year.

To analyze too closely the factors that make for nobility in a life is to confuse them; to dissect a personality too minutely is to lose its image. The qualities that constitute greatness are tantalizing and elusive. But as the theologian Campbell recedes in time, the tremendous figure of Campbell, the man, emerges from the shadows, bigger than life—a man whose heart embraced all Christians as brothers, whose mind was open to all truth, whose eyes had seen the glory of the United Church, and whose influence shall endure until time shall end.

Alexander Campbell and Church Unity

Roland Bainton

Titus Street Professor of Ecclesiastical History at Yale University and author of **The Chuch of Our Fathers**

Alexander Campbell has the singular distinction of being the only Christian reformer whose achievement was the denial of his intention. He sought to unite all of the evangelical churches and instead founded one more. To a degree a similar anomaly is discoverable also in Martin Luther who set out to reform Christendom and ended by rending Christendom. Or again in John Wesley who endeavored to revive the Church of England and headed a secession from the Church of England. Nevertheless, in the case of these latter two, the discrepancy is not so glaring. Luther did reform, even though he divided, and Wesley did revive, even though he seceded. But Alexander Campbell sought to unite and increased division.

The outcome cannot altogether be regarded as a malign trick of a capricious fate. There was something of the same anomaly in the man's deportment, because he sprayed Christian divisions with vitriol. He was an artist in denunciation, ridicule, and satire, and reveled in debate whether with Owen the Infidel, Purcell the Roman Catholic Bishop, or Rice the Infant Baptist. Public disputations in those days were a great popular diversion, the equivalent among the saints of the race track and the prize ring, and Alexander Campbell was a heavy-weight champion. The story is told that Bishop Vardeman, having been selected to moderate a debate in which Campbell was to defend immersion, was traveling in a gig to Washington over a muddy road when he overtook a man on foot and remarked to the traveler that he must have very important business to be trudging to Washington through such weather. The man answered that he was going to hear Campbell debate. Vardeman, suspecting that the man might be on the opposite side, sought to twit him by suggesting that Campbell might whip his champion. The man answered that if this were the Mr. Campbell whom he had heard on a previous occasion then "all creation cannot whip Mr. Campbell."[1]

He was adept at satire which is an admirable weapon in debate, but not often an instrument of conciliation. Here is an example of his counsel to preachers:

> Let your sermon be full of "the enticing words of man's wisdom," and let it be beautified with just divisions, with tropes and with metaphors, and with hyperbole, and apostrophe, and with interrogation, and with acclamation, and with syllogisms, and with sophisms . . . .
>
> And take good heed to your attitudes and your gestures, knowing when to bend and when to erect . . . .

[1]Richardson, *op. cit.*, II, p. 73.

Let your voice at times be smooth as the stream of the valley, and soft as the breeze that waves not the bough on its banks; and at times let it swell like the wave of the ocean, or like the whirlwind on the mountain top.

Then shall you charm the ears of your hearers and their hearts shall be softened, and their minds shall be astounded, and their souls shall incline to you; and the men shall incline to you, and likewise the women; yea, to your sayings and to your persons shall they be inclined.

And be you mindful not to offend the people; rebuke you not their sins . . . .

If a brother shall raise up the banner of war against brother, and christians against christians, rebuke them not . . . .

If any man go into a foreign land and seize upon his fellow man, and put irons on his feet and irons on his hands, and bring him across the great deep into bondage; nay, if he tear asunder the dearest ties of nature, the tenderest leagues of the human heart; if he tear the wife from the husband, and force the struggling infant from its mother's bleeding breast, rebuke him not!

And although he sell them in foreign slavery to toil beneath the lash all their days, tell him not that his doings are of Antichrist; for lo! he is rich and gives to the church.[2]

The first part of this declamation might not have stung since but few would have applied the strictures to themselves, but the castigations on the slave-trade and war might easily have provoked resentment.

This passage is an example of his style. It does not, of course, apply to divisions among Christians. But here is another excerpt which strikes directly at the Baptists, the very group with whom for a time he was in closest affiliation. He is parodying an account of an ordination as given in the Latter Day Luminary. Here is Campbell's rendering:

On Wednesday, the 11th of June, A.D. 44, the Rev. Saulus Paulus and the Rev. Joses Barnabas were set apart as missionaries

[2]*The Christian Baptist,* II, 167-168.

to the Gentiles dispersed throughout the world, by a committee of the board of managers of the Baptist General Convention, met in the city of Antioch. An interesting sermon was delivered on the occasion by the Rev. Simon Niger, from Isaiah xliii, 4. "The isles shall wait for his law." Rev. Lucius of Cyrene led in offering up the consecrating prayer. Rev. Manaen gave Mr. Paulus and his companion (Mr. Barnabas) an appropriate charge; and the Rev. John Mark gave them the right hand of fellowship . . . . The Rev. Lucius of Cyrene offered up the concluding prayer. The services were performed in the Rev. Mr. Simeon Niger's meeting-house. The day was fine, and the assemblage was very large, and proved, by their fixed and silent attention to the services, how much they felt for the world that lieth in wickedness; and by a collection of $86 25 cents, they showed a willingness to aid the Rev. Mr. Paulus and the Rev. Mr. Barnabas in carrying the gospel to the heathen.

Mr. Paulus is a young man, and a native of the city of Tarsus; he received his classical and theological education in the theological seminary in Jerusalem. He appeared before the committee a man of good sense, of ardent piety, and understandingly led by the spirit of God to the work in which he has now engaged.[3]

This passage, to be sure, comes from Campbell's earliest and most acrimonious period. A number of points are pilloried. One is the use of titles for ministers. Reverends and Right Reverends were unknown in the days of Peter and Paul. Will Satan, Campbell demanded, be routed by an army of D.D.'s? (Incidentally, four of the Disciples at Yale have earned the degree of Ph.D. by writing about Alexander Campbell.[4]) Another point was that missionaries should not be paid, that church gatherings should not be in fixed meetinghouses, that ministerial candidates should not receive special training nor should they be conscious of a call from God. Rather, they should be chosen by the congregation on the basis of previous qualifications. Some of these strictures were later to be modified. But the point is that the Baptists

[3]*Ibid.*, I, 1823, edition of 1856, p. 17.

[4]West, *ut supra;* Denton R. Lindley, *The Structure of the Church in the Thought of Alexander Campbell*, 1947, unpublished; Harold L. Lunger, *The Political Ethics of Alexander Campbell* (St. Louis, 1954); Granville T. Walker, *Preaching in the Thought of Alexander Campbell* (St. Louis, 1954).

could scarcely relish his sally any more than his jibe that they had dehorned the beast and produced a hornless ox, still able to maul if not to gore.

As for the Presbyterians, he picked up a notice in one of their journals which lamented "vacant churches deprived of the means of grace." "Oh, Peter! Oh, Paul" Campbell ejaculated, "churches vacant!" How could they be vacant as long as they had members, and how could they be deprived of the means of grace so long as the congregation could appoint one of their own number to administer the Sacraments? However warranted this jibe, the tone was not precisely irenic.

Nevertheless, the failure of Alexander Campbell's efforts for the reunion of the churches is not to be attributed primarily to his attitude. He riddled and ridiculed, but he was not contentious nor cantankerous. Once he ventured to rib an Episcopal minister by branding the affair of Henry VIII and Anne Boleyn as an ugly story. The rector retorted that the Bible contained some ugly stories. Campbell laughed, and arm-in-arm they went in for dinner.[5] Debate and even controversy need not of necessity preclude unity.

Nor again is the work of Alexander for church unity to be written off as vain. Dean Inge once remarked that in religion nothing fails like success, and he might have said that nothing succeeds like failure. A witness is itself of value, and may bear ultimate fruit. Campbell was certainly right in deploring the divisions rampant in his day. He had come from North Ireland where the Presbyterians inherited from Scotland the divisions between the established church and the seceders. And these in turn were split into the Burghers and the Anti-Burghers. This division was crossed by that of the New and the Old Lights to form four parties: New Light Burghers, Old Light Burghers, New Light Anti-Burghers, and Old Light Anti-Burghers. The point between Burghers and Anti-Burghers had reference to an

[5]Richardson, *op. cit.,* II, p. 64.

oath required in Scotland but not in Ireland, let alone in Kentucky. The father of Alexander Campbell, Thomas Campbell, in 1807 came to the United States as the pastor of a Seceder Presbyterian church and when he dared to minister to all varieties of Presbyterians in the area, he was expelled.

Alexander Campbell could not conceive of Christ so divided that there could be a Baptist, Methodist, Presbyterian, Episcopal, and Roman Catholic conscience. (He did not mention the Congregationalists, who did not flourish in his region.) Besides, said he, there is in Kentucky a Licking Association Baptist conscience and a Particular Baptist conscience. Under fictitious names he reported the situation in his district in 1825: "William Pedibus, the shoemaker, lost the custom of all the Presbyterians in town, because he said that Parson Trim denied free agency. And Thomas Vulcanus, the blacksmith, never shod a Methodist's horse since the time he censored Elder Vox's sermon on the possibility of falling from grace."

Campbell lived, as W. E. Garrison has pointed out, when sectarianism had accomplished its work in breaking rigid authoritarianism and tyranny, and had itself become an abuse because of its minute particularism and petty rancor. The time had come to forget or minimize ancient and often outmoded differences and to realize a genuine unity in Christ. If Campbell did found a new denomination, it was a denomination dedicated to Christian unity and has produced a number of noble advocates. A century of exhortation on their part has markedly contributed to the strength of the contemporary ecumenical movement. Another point worthy of note is that Campbell perceived the utter folly of sectarian differences on the mission field, and there it was that the church unity movement had its first inception.

Yet there is no denying that Campbell in his lifetime met with failure. This may be attributed solely to the perversity of the sects, and indeed Campbell said that union required them to "throw away nothing that they possess but error and falsehood."

But then, of course, the question would arise as to what is error and what is falsehood. The failure of his scheme, however, I would suggest lay neither in his own belligerence nor in his opponent's stubbornness, but rather in his formulation of the conditions for unity. The core of his program was epitomized in a slogan already popular: "In essentials unity, in nonessentials liberty, in both charity." The term "essential" referred to that which is necessary to be believed or done as a condition for salvation, and unity meant that on these points no latitude was permissible. All those admitted to the church must agree and conform as to essentials. On matters not requisite for salvation, on which one would not be damned either way, diversity could be allowed, and toward those without as well as toward those within a kindly spirit should be entertained.

This slogan had behind it a long history.[6] St. Augustine had long since recognized a distinction between points of greater and lesser importance and quoted with relish the retort to one who asked what God was doing before he created the world; namely, that he was making hell for those who asked too many questions. On the eve of the Reformation the Brethren of the Common Life employed the idea in order to disparage theological speculation. Their patron saint was the Penitent Thief who was saved with so little theology. He believed only that Christ could get him to Paradise. Erasmus of Rotterdam in this tradition recommended deferring to the judgment day the discussion of thorny and insoluble riddles, such as the distinction between the generation of the Son and procession of the Holy Ghost, or as to how God could be both three and one. That alone, said Erasmus, can be essential for salvation which can be universally understood and the emphasis should be placed on the fruits of the spirit rather than on the tenets of the head. Sebastian Castellio, in the great controversy over the execution of Servetus for heresy, ventured to

[6]Walter Koehler, "Die Geistesahnen des Acontius," *Festschrift für Karl Müller* (Tübingen, 1922), pp. 198-208.

classify among the nonessentials the belief in the Trinity and predestination, as well as an opinion as to whether Christ was ubiquitous as Luther held, or seated at the right hand of God the Father as Zwingli and Calvin contended. But the man who gave the idea its most influential formulation was Jacob Acontius in a book entitled *The Wiles of Satan*. He there affirmed that alone to be essential to salvation which is so designated in Scripture and he could discover only two points. "The just shall live by faith." Therefore they are excluded who live by works and this rules out the Catholics. The other text is "Believe on the Lord Jesus Christ and you shall be saved." This would exclude the Sabellians and one would have thought also the Socinians, though Acontius did not draw this conclusion. He broke a lance for Anabaptists who adopted a Gnostic attitude as to the flesh of Christ, not on the ground that they were right but that the point was not essential for salvation.

One observes that the principle of unity in essentials and liberty in nonessentials is exclusive as well as inclusive. Only those who unite on essentials can be admitted and only they may enjoy liberty as to nonessentials. The outworking of the principle is strikingly illustrated in the scheme of Oliver Cromwell who, in line with the idea of Acontius, excluded the Catholics and the Unitarians. He included in the following order of preference the Congregationalists, Baptists, and Presbyterians with the Anglicans and Quakers on the fringe subject to restriction primarily on political grounds because the Anglicans adhered to the crown and the Quakers would not fight against the king.

Alexander Campbell had the same basic plan and he defined the essentials in the same manner. With Acontius he held that the points necessary for salvation can be only those so stipulated in the New Testament. This is our sole source of the knowledge of God. This is, as it were, the charter of the church. We are to "open the New Testament as if mortal man had never seen it before," casting aside all preconceived notions, all sophisticated subtleties, all creeds which are merely inferences from the Bible and therefore the inventions of men. If we thus open the Book we shall find two conditions for salvation. Said Campbell: "THE BELIEF OF ONE FACT . . . *is all that is requisite, as far as faith goes, to salvation. The belief of this* ONE FACT, *and submission to* ONE INSTITUTION *expressive of it, is all that is required of Heaven to admission into the church.* . . . The one fact is expressed in a single proposition—*that Jesus the Nazarene is the Messiah* . . . the *one institution* is baptism into the name of the Father, and of the Son, and the Holy Spirit."[7] Observe that there is an article of belief. Campbell did not object to a creed, for any article of faith is a creed. Neither did he object to the use of a creed as a test. His objection was to any creed which goes beyond the Bible. In addition to belief he postulated one demand as to practice, namely, baptism.

If Campbell had stopped here he might have had a basis on which a very large degree of union could have been possible. The Universalists would not have been excluded. Campbell considered them mistaken though no worse than those who think that hell holds infants not a span long. Both have "mounted their winged horse and soared beyond the regions of revelation." He defended the right of a Universalist named Raines to Christian fellowship because he advanced Universalism as a private opinion and not as a part of the gospel. Such tolerance was considered to have been vindicated when Raines later renounced his error.

The demands above formulated by Campbell would not have excluded the Unitarians. Many of them would have confessed that Jesus was the Messiah. They might have balked at baptism in the name of the Father, the Son, and the Holy Ghost, though these terms could have been defined in a New Testament rather than in a Nicene sense. Campbell affirmed that he would not reject a man because he was a Unitarian, if he would confess that Jesus of Nazareth is the Messiah, the Son of God. On the

[7]*The Christian System,* p. 101.

other hand, the Socinians whom he defined as those who called Jesus the son of Joseph, he described not as Christians but as "drivelling philosophers." And he went on to say, "From my heart I pity these Socinians . . . and would not, the Bible being in my hand, rush into the presence of the Judge of quick and dead with their sentiments, for twice the value of the universe."[8]

The conditions as stipulated above are certainly broad. But then Campbell began by definition and addition to narrow the range. Baptism, said he, meant only adult baptism. In the New Testament he could find no reference to infant baptism, therefore it could not have been practiced and therefore it is not to be observed by us. With one stroke he cut off the possibility of union with all of the churches except the Baptists, unless, of course, the others were to abandon their own tenets. As for those who did not, said he: "Infants, idiots, deaf and dumb persons, innocent Pagans . . . with all the pious Pedobaptists, we commend to the mercy of God. But such of them as willfully *despise* this salvation, and who, having the opportunity to be immersed for the remission of their sins, willfully *despise* or refuse, we have as little hope for them as they have for all who refuse salvation *on their own terms of the gospel.*"[9]

Next he arrived at the conclusion that the term "baptize" in the New Testament could mean only immersion. He found no record of sprinkling; therefore there was no sprinkling. And if immersion was the universal mode, then the New Testament verse should be translated "Repent and be immersed." Immersion is necessary to salvation because only in this way are we in actual possession of the remission of our sins. The nonimmersed may indeed be happy in the peace of God because they are not aware that they are lost, but none can enjoy a rational hope save those immersed for the remission of sins. On the other

---

[8] *The Christian Baptist,* p. 51.
[9] *The Christian System,* p. 203.

hand, both as to adult baptism and immersion as absolute conditions for salvation or even church union there was some wavering.

At another time he said, "There is no occasion for making immersion on a profession of faith absolutely essential to a Christian." Again he declared that there are pedobaptist congregations "of whose christianity, . . . I think as highly, as of most Baptist congregations, and with whom I could wish to be on the very same terms of christian communion on which I stand with the whole Baptist society."

His tendency was, however, to grow more and more restrictive. There were two principles operative in his procedure. One was to return to the simplicity of the New Testament faith and require no more. The other was to restore the practice of the Early Christian community and to suffer no less. A further assumption was that the practice of the New Testament churches must have been uniform. Campbell noted in the Book of Acts (20:7) the verse which read that at Troas "On the first day of the week when the disciples came together for the breaking of the loaf." The purpose of the assembly then was to celebrate the Lord's Supper. What was done on that first day must have been done on every first day, and what was done at Troas must have been done in every Christian community. And what then constituted the universal practice of the early church is binding, likewise, upon present-day Christians. Whether Campbell intended to say that the observance of this practice is necessary for salvation is not clear. He did consider it necessary for church membership and presumably also for Christian unity. He may have shifted his definition of essential from that which is essential for salvation to that which is necessary for unity. In any case, he had introduced a further restrictive principle. In fact, he had reached the point where he could not unite with anybody. The insistence on adult baptism cut off all save the Baptists, and weekly communion eliminated them. Campbell had ended up with a new denomination.

What then of church unity? It is not entirely clear that he desired it any more. He declared, as a matter of fact, quite early in his career, "I have no idea of seeing, nor one wish to see, the sects unite in one grand army. This would be dangerous to our liberties and laws. For this the Saviour did not pray."[10] Is then the ideal that there should be denominations, but that they should cherish each other in a spirit of charity? Organic unity would then be relinquished as an ideal.

He noted the possibility of fellowship at different levels. Already there were Baptists and pedobaptists who met together in monthly meetings for prayer and praise, yet they were not willing to take communion together. He agreed that baptism must precede communion, and of course baptism administered in the proper way. Still it was an anomaly to be willing to pray and praise in unison and not to sit down at the Lord's Table. He seemed unsettled in his own mind, whether to remove the disparity by moving forward to the Lord's Table or by going in the other direction to cut off the joint prayer meetings.

When one surveys Campbell's life work now, it may seem pathetic because he decried the haggling of the sects and yet set up such conditions for Christian unity that none could unite save those who adopted a system different from that of all the rest. It is easy enough to pick flaws and discover inconsistencies in his scheme. His assumption that New Testament practice was uniform is entirely untenable and one wonders why on his own premises he did not go on to daily communion, because we read in the Book of Acts that "the disciples continued daily in breaking bread." Campbell got around this by making a distinction between the Lord's Supper and the love feast. But for this separation there is no warrant prior to the second century. In any case, the entire effort to discover a uniform pattern in early

[10] *The Christian Baptist,* p. 140.

Christian practice has proved untenable by modern historical research.

Consequently, we cannot go back to Alexander Campbell for a specific scheme of church unity, but we can learn from him. And one thing we can learn is his willingness to learn. He changed a great deal during his lifetime. He confessed that once he had been like the Indian's tree, so straight that it leaned a little the other way. His opposition to missionary societies and to a trained ministry was abandoned after he became the leader of a new denomination. In fact, his whole program suffered change. One writer has suggested that until 1830 his effort was to unite the churches, that from 1830 'til his death the plan was to draw the receptive out of the unreformed churches. A third stage came after his death when the Disciples became a denomination and took their place as colleagues with mutual respect for the others. That stage may not have been reached by Alexander Campbell, but he was on the way. He was never static. His very progress, of course, may be regarded as an abandonment of his ideal of unity. And yet that was not the case. He never ceased to lament sectarianism. Just what better scheme we can devise to overcome it, is for us to work out. We are indebted to him for a persistent harping on the scandal, not only of division, but of acrimony.

The greatest thing about the man was his spirit. Commenting on his debate with the Presbyterians, he said:

> I have no object but truth, and whatever may be published against my pamphlet, in a christian and candid manner, shall receive every attention. But let them not lose their temper, nor substitute railing for argument. . . . If any are convinced, let them beware of stifling convictions . . . .
>
> Though I am decidedly convinced of the complete independency of the apostolical churches, and of the duty of following them, I would not be understood as placing undue importance upon this point. Christians of every denomination I love; and I will never,

I hope, withhold my hand, or my countenance from any who, after impartial investigation, conscientiously differ from me. I can from my heart say, "Grace be with all those who love our Lord Jesus Christ in sincerity and truth."[11]

[11]*Ibid.*, p. 75.

Alexander Campbell's Views on Baptism in the Light of the Ecumenical Movement

STEPHEN J. ENGLAND

Dean of the Divinity School at Phillips University and author of **The One Baptism**

Introduction

On June 12, 1812, Alexander Campbell, who had been brought up in the Seceder Presbyterian Chuch and who had received christening as an infant in that faith, was baptized by immersion in the waters of Buffalo Creek. This action, deliberately undertaken, was the first in a momentous chain of events.

Campbell was at the time serving the Brush Run church as minister. Immediately he became known as a Baptist minister and his church as a Baptist church. Because Campbell was a man of towering intellectual stature and superb public-speaking ability, he became the champion of the Baptist position in debates with certain Presbyterian ministers. That is, he defended the action of immersion as baptism and believers as the only proper subjects to be baptized. While Campbell's able defense of this position was well liked by his fellow ministers among the Baptists, he brought up two arguments to support these positions which led to tension between him and the Baptists. The proponents of infant baptism held that just as infants were circumcized under the regulations of the Old Testament, so infants should be baptized under the Church as revealed in the New Testament. Mr. Campbell attacked this position by attempting to show the clear distinction between the old covenant and the new convenant. Such a division within the pages of Holy Writ was very distasteful to the Baptist churches among which he moved.

Mr. Campbell also upheld the position that only believers should be baptized by developing the teaching of the New Testament that baptism was for the remission of past sins, actually committed. Because many if not most of the Baptist churches held that baptism followed the forgiveness of sins rather than preceding it, they disliked Mr. Campbell's argument while applauding the victorious results. As the outcome of these debates, tensions began to develop between Mr. Campbell and the increasing number of churches which followed him on the one side and the regular Baptist churches among which he moved on the other.

Growing directly out of his debates with Walker and Maccalla came the tremendous evangelistic success of Walter Scott. Mr. Campbell had taught that faith is basically the acceptance of the evidence that Jesus is the Messiah. Joining this concept of faith with the teaching that baptism is for the remission of sins, thus making the act of baptism both the climax of the conversion experience and the positive assurance of pardon, Walter Scott developed an evangelistic message of tremendous power. Beginning in 1826 in the communities of Western Pennsylvania, Eastern Ohio, and Northern Kentucky this evangelism spread like an uncontrolled prairie fire. The tremendous multiplication of congregations and members holding these views was a principal cause of the separation of Mr. Campbell from the Baptist fellowship.

When the separation finally occurred and the new group calling themselves "Disciples of Christ" became recognizable as a distinct religious body, they were proudly and militantly immersionist. They would accept Christians from other churches upon transfer only on the basis of baptism by immersion. The doctrine of baptism for remission of sins was a chief theological characteristic of the new group.

The act of Alexander Campbell in June, 1812, thus eventuated within twenty years the formation of a new religious group among whom baptism was a very important doctrine and practice.

Baptism was also important to Mr. Campbell himself. He engaged in five major debates. In the first two, against Walker and Maccalla, baptism was the only topic discussed. In the last, with Nathan L. Rice, the discussion of baptism occupies over 600 pages out of the 900-odd pages of the volume which reports the debates. In his periodical writings, which extended over a period beginning in 1823 when he first began publication of *The Christian Baptist* and running through the pages of the later periodical, the *Millennial Harbinger,* the topic of baptism recurs with great frequency. Mr. Campbell himself collected a number of these articles and edited them for republication in a volume of 441 pages under the title of *Christian Baptism, Its Antecedents and Consequents.* The one formal volume which Mr. Campbell published concerning his doctrines bears the title *The Christian System.* In this, only four pages deal formally with the topic of baptism. There are, however, other incidental references in the same volume. In all his writings both in the periodicals and in the *Christian System* Campbell made it plain that the discussion of baptism was in the interest not only of the restoration of primitive Christianity but also of the union and unity of Christians.

Some of the present-day leaders among Disciples of Christ have felt somewhat apologetic about Campbell's emphasis upon baptism. Among these, the tendency is to hold that baptism is really not important to unity, and that the problem presented by divergences in the practice of baptism among Christian groups can best be solved simply by neglecting their existence or by accepting them without question. In some quarters there is a tendency to feel that there is something a little uncharitable and un-Christian in discussing baptism within groups where there are divergent views and that especially to raise any questions as to immersion or to baptism of infants is at best discourteous, and is at worst an attempt to make trouble.

It is a striking fact that the views of those who would minimize the importance of baptism are so little supported in modern scholarship and especially within the Ecumenical Movement. Within recent times baptism has become a lively topic of theological discussion. Among the more recent authors we may list Karl Barth, whose book in German in 1943 was translated in 1948 into English under the title *The Teaching of the Church Regarding Baptism*. A response to Barth, written by Oscar Cullmann in German in 1948, was translated into English in 1952 under the title *Baptism in the New Testament*. The church of Scotland has become so interested in baptism that it appointed a Special Commission on Baptism which has been publishing interim reports annually since 1955. The World Council of Churches has taken notice of this interest by publishing a selected bibliography which in 1957 listed twelve titles in English, ten in German, and two in French. In July, 1957, just prior to the North American Conference on Faith and Order at Oberlin, Ohio, the Faith and Order Commission of the World Council of Churches held a meeting at New Haven, Connecticut. One of the documents presented there was entitled "A Working Paper on Baptism." This was presented for discussion before the group together with comments by a subcommittee. At the Oberlin Conference, one Section studied "Baptism into Christ." The official report of the Section stated six objectives of its study, four of which seem to have relevance to the topic of this paper. They are:

a. to discover the extent to which Christian baptism is an element in our unity and disunity.
b. To listen together to Scripture for its teaching concerning the power of baptism to unify God's people.
c. To discern the recent changes in both scholarly and popular attitudes toward the significance of this event.
d. to examine the degree of consensus in the doctrine and practice of baptism which is necessary before greater unity can be realized.[1]

In the light of such a statement, the position of Alexander Campbell is justified at least thus far: baptism has an important relation to the achievement of unity. It is impossible to think of moving forward into Christian unity without some "consensus in the doctrine and practice of baptism." This is obviously an appropriate time to take a new look at Campbell's doctrine and practice of baptism, in the light of the present trend in the Ecumenical Movement.

The Doctrine of Baptism, in Campbell and in the Modern Ecumenical Movement

It requires only a casual glance at Campbell's writings on baptism to remind us that to him his doctrine of baptism

[1]*The Nature of the Unity We Seek: Official Report of the North American Conference on Faith and Order,* edited by Paul S. Minear, 1958, pp. 194ff.

meant "What is taught in the New Testament?" He would doubtless have applauded the statement of the Section at Oberlin which desired "to listen together to Scripture for its teachings," rather than starting with "our contemporary denominational habits," as the Faith and Order group remarked in the New Haven meeting of 1957.

1. The Form of Baptism

Alexander Campbell asserted that, in the New Testament, only immersion in water was the action called "baptism." His three opponents in debate attempted to show that effusion or sprinkling could equally be found in the New Testament. In the support of his position, Campbell was superb. He adduced the evidence from Greek lexicons. He analyzed root and derivative meanings of Greek words. He cited the fathers of the Church from the earliest generations onward. He brought together the comments of leading Pedobaptist scholars. As Campbell pointed out, the evidence at this point is almost overwhelming, and Campbell's handling of the topic has by no means been superseded. Modern scholarship has almost unanimously agreed that, in the New Testament, only immersion was practiced as baptism. While the discussions of the Ecumenical Movement have not progressed to the point of listening together to Scripture for its teachings, as to the action which the New Testament called "baptism," recent writings seem to indicate clearly enough what the decision will be. For example, Karl Barth[2] writes,

> Is the last word to be that facility of administration, health and propriety are important reasons for doing otherwise [than administer immersion]? Or will a Christianity return whose more vigorous administration will no longer be satisfied with the innocuous form of present-day baptism? The custom followed in

[2]Barth, Karl: *The Teaching of the Church Regarding Baptism;* London, S. C. M. Press, 1948, pp. 9f.

baptism is to be called good or bad as it more or less adequately represents [a death and a return to life?]

That this judgment is not unanimous may be illustrated, however, by a statement from the Special Commission on Baptism of the Church of Scotland:[3]

The language used in the New Testament does not necessarily imply that baptism was by immersion. Certainly the people descended into the water and again ascended out of it; but they may have descended up to their breasts and had water poured upon their heads, as some examples of early Christian art indicate.

This argument is hardly convincing, from either the practical or the scholarly viewpoint. It would be difficult to find a scholarly commentary on the New Testament which would give serious consideration to such a view.

It is an interesting tribute to the scholarship of Alexander Campbell that he upheld a position now so generally accepted. Those who came immediately after Campbell, and some who came later, even down to our own time, felt that the debate over the New Testament form of the ceremony touched the essential issue. These believed that if agreement could be reached that only immersion was practiced in New Testament times, agreement would be automatic as to the modern practice of baptism. Regardless of how important one may regard a decision concerning this New Testament teaching, it is obvious that the attempt to rest everything on the decision as to the form is but a superficial attack on the modern problem.

Campbell seems not to have come to a definite conclusion on one of the basic points: the relation of the form of the ceremony to its meaning and its validity; and the modern Ecumenical Movement has not yet attacked this problem. If the New Testament knew only immersion as baptism, one of the important questions is this: Is immersion essential to baptism? Can the

[3]*Interim Report of the Special Committee on Baptism*, May, 1955; pp. 15f.

"one baptism" (Eph. 4:5) be administered without immersion? Campbell's statements in this regard are not definite nor or they consistent. In 1830 he wrote, "There is no immersion instituted by Jesus Christ, save that *for the remission of sins.* This, and this only, is the '*one immersion.*'" It is not quite clear whether he referred to the form or the meaning of the rite as the essential item. Later, he wrote, "There is, then, but one baptism, and not two, under the Christian administration," in a context which refers to immersion as the action. On the contrary, in 1837 he wrote,

> Can he who, through a simple mistake, involving no perversity of mind, has misapprehended the outward baptism, yet submitting to it according to his view of it, have the inward baptism which changes his state and has praise of God, though not of all men? is the precise question. To which I answer, that, in my opinion, *it is possible.*[4]

Campbell was evidently not willing to restrict the religious effectiveness of baptism to the form employed.

2. The Subjects of Baptism

Campbell's position, taken in three of his great debates, was that in the New Testament only those who had made a profession of faith were admitted to baptism. In handling the evidence on this point, Campbell again displayed his superlative abilities. His interpretation of the New Testament passages where infant baptism is supposedly referred to has not been outdated. His citations from the church fathers as to the history of the introduction of the practice are excellent. In particular, his devastating attack upon the argument of his Pedobaptist opponents, that infant baptism must have been practiced among the Jews, still stands as the most thorough treatment of this

[4]*Millennial Harbinger,* 1837, p. 507.

topic. It is a reasoned judgment to say that Campbell successfully established his position, that infants were not admitted to baptism by the Church in New Testament times.

The question of the proper subjects of baptism has also been discussed in modern scholarship, and has now been introduced into the Ecumenical Movement. Insofar as the discussions relate to the practice in New Testament times, there is general though not unanimous agreement that in the New Testament, infants were not baptized. Among the important dissenters at this point we may cite the Special Commission on Baptism of the Church in Scotland, whose report finds infants invited to baptism in Acts 2:39, where "children" are referred to; and by setting Matthew 18:1 and Matthew 19:13 in a liturgical context, discovers infant baptism. Oscar Cullmann admits that infant baptism could hardly have occurred in the very beginning of the Church. In the time of beginnings, the response of faith was essential to the setting up of the New Christian community, in distinction from Judaism. He goes on, however, to argue that the "mission situation" was not the normative life of the church. As soon as the response of faith had led to the formation of Christian communities, and as soon as children were born into Christian families, Cullmann believes that such infants must have been admitted to baptism. He would thus conclude that while the evidence in the New Testament is decisively against the practice, this should not govern the life of the church in succeeding generations. He supports his contention for the early rise of the custom of infant baptism by the familiar argument, "The doctrine and practice of circumcision are presuppositions for the whole complicated question of New Testament baptismal doctrine and practice."[5]

With this, Barth decisively disagrees. In language controverting infant baptism as sharply as anything Alexander Campbell ever wrote, he asserts, "Baptism in the New Testament in

[5]Cullmann, O.: *Baptism in the New Testament;* Chicago, Henry Regnery Co., 1950.

every case is the indispensable answer to an unavoidable question by one who had come to faith." After rejecting Matthew 19:13 as giving no evidence concerning baptism (a position which Campbell had asserted a century earlier), Barth cites Matthew 28:19 to show that one must be "discipled" before he may be admitted to baptism. Rejecting Colossians 2:11 and its reference to circumcision as irrelevant to the question, he says, "from the New Testament standpoint it is impossible to say that everyone who is born of Christian parents is born into the Christian Church." Barth takes no stock whatever in the so-called "household baptisms" of Acts as supporting the practice of infant baptism. Thus he says, "the case for a New Testament proof of infant baptism is more than weak." Summarizing his conclusions from the study of the New Testament, Barth says, with devastating sharpness, "from the standpoint of a doctrine of baptism, infant baptism can hardly be preserved without exegetical and practical artifices and sophisms. One wants to preserve it only if one is resolved to do so on grounds which lie outside the biblical passages, and outside the thing itself."[6]

Within the Ecumenical Movement, The Faith and Order Commission of the World Council of Churches, meeting at New Haven in July, 1957, gave brief consideration to the matter of infant baptism. The approach was not direct, but dealt incidentally with infant baptism in the relation, first, of baptism to an individual profession of faith, and, second, of baptism to Christian nurture. While no definite statement issued from the Oberlin deliberations, the question underlay the discussions, and must emerge more clearly into the open in later gatherings.

3. The Administrator of Baptism

The question of the administrator of baptism is only casually introduced into Campbell's writings. In the last of his great de-

[6]Barth, *op. cit.*, pp. 42-48, *passim.*

bates, that with Rice, Campbell affirmed that "ordination by imposition of hands is not essential to the validity of the church's ordinances." When the debate was joined on this issue, there seemed to be little if any difference between the debators. The discussion was limited to the minor issue of what would be for the good order of the Christian community. While Campbell asserted that the validity of baptism (or any other ordinance) did not depend upon the ordination of the one administering, he agreed that it was proper to restrict the administration to those who could and would do so with propriety and decency; and with this, Rice agreed.

Within the Ecumenical Movement, there has been little discussion of the proper administrator of baptism. This is no doubt due to two circumstances. The discussion of baptism has hardly proceeded beyond introducing the topic; and the question of who may properly or validly administer baptism is related to the similar and perhaps more pressing problem of who may properly and validly conduct the communion service. The issue here involves the order of the church. If an agreement can be reached in regard to the proper administrator of the communion, doubtless the administration of baptism will be included. We should not deceive ourselves, however, by supposing that the problem here is an easy or inconsequential one. The Faith and Order Commission, meeting at New Haven in July, 1957, noted that the questions of the persons by whom, through whom, and to whom the authority for baptism is given must be dealt with.

4. The Meaning of Baptism

To a considerable degree, Campbell's discussion of the meaning or purpose, or (as he said) "design" of baptism, as seen in the New Testament, deals with a doctrine characteristic of Disciples of Christ: "baptism for the remission of sins." As a matter of history, Campbell seems to have developed the statement of the doctrine in his debate with Maccalla, in 1823, as a supporting argument against supposing that infants were baptized in the New Testament Church. He later developed the doctrine very greatly, so that no theological position is more emphasized in his writings. For example, he wrote, "No one is commanded to be baptized *for any thing else;* and no one is ever said to have been baptized *for any thing else,* than for the remission of sins." Probably because there is so much in the New Testament that supports this view, Campbell devoted surprisingly little space to other possible interpretations of the purpose of baptism; although, in the volume on *Christian Baptism,* he lists, as "consequents" of baptism, "justification, sanctification and adoption."

Campbell tried to guard himself against misunderstanding of his affirmation that "baptism is for the remission of past sins," and in particular, against the charge that he believed in "water salvation." He did not utterly succeed. He defended himself in these forthright words: "Baptism . . . has no abstract efficacy. Without previous faith in the blood of Christ and deep and unfeigned repentance before God, neither immersion in water nor any other action, can secure to us the blessings of peace and pardon." Considerably earlier, in the debate with Maccalla, he said, "The water of baptism, then, *formally* washes away our sins. The blood of Christ *really* washes away our sins. Paul's sins were *really pardoned* when he believed, yet he had no solemn *pledge* of the fact . . . until he washed them away in the water of baptism." Despite these precautions, Campbell was repeatedly accused of teaching "baptismal regeneration." Some of Campbell's more rigorous followers, even down to our time, seem unaware of Campbell's careful statements in this connection. Campbell did not believe that immersion in water as baptism is essential to salvation. Yet the ancient accusation as to the belief of Disciples of Christ concerning the relation of baptism to salvation still persists. No longer than a decade ago, union negotiations with the Northern Baptists foundered in part upon the belief among the Baptist group that Christian Churches of today hold to "water salvation."

It is not difficult to discover affirmations in writers earlier than Campbell who agree that baptism is related to the forgiveness of sins; nor is it difficult to discover similar statements within the Ecumenical Movement. From Oberlin, in 1957, came the following: "In baptism . . . must be interpreted as response to what God has already done in Christ. . . . Any interpretation of baptism, which reduces it merely to a sign of human commitment or testimony, leaves out of account an essential element in the New Testament conception of baptism."[7] The modern discussions differ from Campbell chiefly in the relative emphasis on "baptism for forgiveness," and in their introducing and elaborating upon other meanings of baptism.

In summary, we should not forget that Campbell's approach to the doctrine of baptism was almost exclusively from the viewpoint of the New Testament. To him, the authentic doctrine of baptism was simply what the New Testament said about it, or reported concerning its practice. Committed as he was to the attempt to "restore the ancient order of things" as a prelude to union and unity, he could not have been expected to proceed differently.

The Practice of Baptism, in Campbell and in the Modern Ecumenical Movement

1. Background and Atmosphere

Like those with whom he debated, Alexander Campbell approached his study of baptism from the viewpoint that the New

[7]Minear, *op. cit.*, p. 196.

Testament is not only normative, it is the divine directive, so that whatever was required by God of those to whom the gospel was first preached is required in the Church forever. In the case of baptism, when Campbell discovered that the New Testament mentions only immersion as the act of baptism, and leaves no record that infants were baptized, he assumed that in his day believers should be immersed, and that their infant children were not eligible to baptism.

Furthermore, Campbell can be understood only if we remember that he was the iconoclast and the reformer, whose characterization of his movement was "the current reformation." Because he was the reformer, challenging and attacking what he considered the errors and defect of the church in his time, he had no *status quo* to defend. He did not hesitate to strike forth into new areas. He was not bound by any opinions held before him. Consistently, he did not hesitate to follow personally what he advocated for others. When he became convinced that in the New Testament baptism was immersion and that infants were not properly subjects of baptism, he presented himself for immersion at the hands of a Baptist minister, although he had received sprinkling as an infant and had been preaching in the Brush Run Church for some time.

Both Campbell's outlook on the New Testament and his bold and ruthless attack upon precedent made it difficult for those in the middle of the twentieth century to approach the subject of baptism as he did. Even Disciples of Christ now have behind them more than a century of habits and practices of their own group, which are difficult to throw off. The modern view of the New Testament does not readily agree that its specific admonitions are to be specifically obeyed as the voice of God, and even those who regard the New Testament as normative are usually unwilling to go to the length of detailed obedience which Campbell proposed. The present-day descendants of Campbell are not so much reformers as they are churchmen, responsible for maintaining and preserving the values which have accumulated during the years of their heritage. They, no less than their religious neighbors, find it hardly possible to launch out without regard to the past in the same way that Campbell did.

It is also true that Campbell's teaching and practice of baptism were conceived and nurtured in the atmosphere of religious controversy with results that were not entirely fortunate. Campbell developed his understanding of baptism largely against those who opposed. Because he saw so clearly the need for reform, he stated his case more strongly than he might have done had the atmosphere been less highly charged. When he stood on the platform to debate on baptism, the immediate need to win may have been more prominent than the desire to discover the truth. On the other side, also, it is possible that his opponents may have stated their opposition more strongly than the case required, simply because it was in the atmosphere of controversy, leading Campbell to attack their positions and defend his own with increased vigor and perhaps some lack of balance. This is not to imply that Campbell perverted his sense of truth in order to win; it is to suggest that controversy demands an emphasis which calm and sober discussion might eliminate. If the modern ecumenical movement is now to proceed in calm discussions among those who are determined to learn the will of God for the church of our time, we may come to a considerably greater degree of agreement in regard to baptism than was possible in Campbell's lifetime.

This should not blunt our discernment of the fact that Campbell always carried out his discussions of baptism in the light of his deep desire for the union of the Christians. Whatever he advocated, he believed firmly that it led in the desired direction. His practice of baptism may be considered in the light of these assumptions.

2. The Children of Believers

The churches that Campbell led held that the New Testament taught only immersion as the action of baptism; hence, they administered only immersion to those making profession of faith. They believed that the New Testament knew nothing of baptism for those unable to make such profession; hence, they refused to baptize infants.

Since these churches grew up out of controversy with Pedobaptist bodies, it was natural that they should reject anything that looked like infant baptism. So Campbell wrote, in 1846, that he wanted nothing to do with "infant dedication," meaning a religious ceremony that committed the helpless child, in advance, to the religious position of its parents, especially if that was in a "sectarian" church. By this decision, Campbell did not entirely solve the problem of what the church ought to do about the children of believers, and Disciples of Christ have inherited a resulting embarrassment. The difficulty arises because there has been no systematic provision for the nurture of the child, leading up to the time when a profession of faith can be made. The result is that oftentimes a local church finds itself facing the urgent demand of the six-year-old child of Christian parents who desire baptism on the ground that he can repeat the words of the good confession. This may be nothing more than infant baptism by subterfuge. Administering the rite to those of too tender years may effectually prevent such instruction as would lead to a great experience of commitment of life to Christ in more mature years.

3. Receiving the Unimmersed Members of Other Churches

It was Campbell's practice of requiring unimmersed members to submit to immersion, if they transferred membership, which stirred opposition and resentment in his day. His opponents called this "rebaptism." Campbell insisted that those who had received sprinkling had never been baptized, insofar as the form was concerned, and that, therefore, this was simply "baptism." Churches of Disciples of Christ have in general followed the lead of Campbell not only in administering only immersion and refusing to baptize infants, but also in the requirement of immersion as the sole basis of membership. In the last item, however, a number of churches have dissented from Campbell's position, preferring to practice the so-called "open membership." By this is meant, in general, the practice of receiving members of other churches with no requirement of any baptism in addition to that already received.

It is at the point of the exchange of members among churches that the consideration of practical steps leading to the union of Christians in the ecumenical movement becomes urgent. The Oberlin report recognizes the problem, but the solution is by no means clearly stated.

Modern Pedobaptist scholars are no nearer accepting the position of Campbell than were their predecessors in Campbell's day. Karl Barth may be taken as an example, the more significant because, as we have seen above, he holds that only immersion was practiced in the New Testament; that a return to immersion is greatly to be desired; and that infants were not baptized in New Testament times. Barth says, "No rejection of the order and practice of baptism through the fault of the Church, or through the fault or lack on the part of the candidate, can make the baptism of a person, once it has been performed, ineffective or invalid, or can lead to or justify a call to re-baptize according to a better order and practice."[8] Barth holds that the nature, power, and meaning of baptism are fundamentally independent of the order and practice. The Oberlin report, recognizing the diversities in practice of the various churches, gives

[8]Barth, *op. cit.*, p. 49.

no hint that there will be unification by adopting any one practice of baptism.

In summary, we may note that Campbell's doctrine of baptism has won substantial support in the modern world, and his position that baptism is closely linked to unity is that of the ecumenical movement. It is the practice of baptism which is marked by the greatest divergence. That divergence is widest where it concerns the case that could not have arisen in the New Testament Church; that is, what should be done about those members of churches who have not received the form of baptism described in the New Testament, or who have been admitted to baptism prior to making a profession of faith? There were evidently no such persons in the scene of the New Testament Church. Yet the present-day ecumenical movement attempts to unite these church members with others who have held strictly to New Testament practice. A decision as to the practice of baptism which will serve to unite these groups cannot be reached on the simple basis of New Testament precedent, for the case did not arise until long after the New Testament was written. Since Campbell believed his practice of baptism was the direct way to union, an analytical look at the practice is the more important.

Campbell's Views on Baptism in Relation to Unity

As we have seen above, Campbell believed that his advocacy of baptism, on the basis he proposed, was a straight way to the uniting of divided Christians. It has been widely held, on the contrary, that this was the weakest part of his plan. A modern historian of the movement says, "The adoption of immersion . . ., as the unvarying practice of the church and therefore as an item in the proposed platform for the union of all churches radically changed the program of the movement."[9] In Camp-

[9]R. H. Bainton in "Alexander Campbell and Christian Unity."

bell's lifetime, Barton W. Stone, leader of a movement that merged with that of Campbell, wrote in 1830,

> Should they [Campbell's followers] make their own peculiar views of immersion a term of fellowship, it will be impossible for them to repel, successfully, the imputation of being sectarians, and of having an authoritative creed (though not written) of one article at least, which is formed of their own opinion of truth; and this short creed would exclude more christians from union than any creed with which I am acquainted.[10]

In 1843 Nathan L. Rice, Campbell's opponent in his last great debate, quoted Stone with approval. In our own time, Roland H. Bainton of the Yale Divinity School, eminent teacher of Church History, holds that Campbell's position on baptism narrowed the range of stipulations as to union. Bainton includes in the difficulties the restriction of baptism to adults; the definition of baptism in the New Testament as only immersion; and holding that immersion is necessary to salvation. As we shall see below, Campbell did not hold the last view.

In the face of this impressive array of negative evaluations, we may look again at the implications of Campbell's position in regard to baptism, as it related then, and still relates, to the possibility of union. During his career three implications were drawn from his statements and practices, and the same three persist in our time. The basic question, then as now, is the religious status of those who received only sprinkling as baptism, including especially those who were admitted to baptism as infants. Does their status require them to receive immersion as a basis for union?

One implication has been drawn by the group of rigorists who stand in the line of succession of Alexander Campbell, and their position has been attributed to him. To those rigorists, the problem and its solution are simple. Baptism is immersion, hence, to be unimmersed is to be unbaptized and to be unbaptized (that is,

---

[10] *Millennial Harbinger*, 1830, pp. 370f.

unimmersed) is to be unforgiven. The only conclusion to be drawn from the presence of unimmersed members of churches is that they are not Christians. Since they are not Christians, they need baptism.

Whatever else this position may be, it is not a plan for the union of Christians. If the unimmersed are for that reason not Christians, then this is a plan for converting pagans, not for uniting Christians. As a matter of fact, this view leads logically to the sacramentarian interpretation of baptism. Denying the evidence that one who displays the image of Christ is a Christian, it holds that to immerse such a person in water almost magically transforms him from an unbeliever into a Christian. It is this view which has led to the modern accusation that "Campbellites believe in water salvation." This position, although attributed to Alexander Campbell, was definitely rejected by him. In 1837 he wrote,

> There is no occasion, then, for making immersion, on a profession of faith, absolutely essential to a Christian—though it may be greatly essential to his sanctification and comfort. My right hand and my right eye are greatly essential to my usefulness and happiness, but not to my life; and as I could not be a perfect man without them, so I cannot be a perfect Christian without a right understanding and cordial reception of immersion in its true and scriptural meaning and design. But he that thence infers that none are Christians but the immersed, as greatly errs as he who affirms that none are alive but those of clear and full vision.[11]

A second implication drawn from Campbell's position was that of the Pedobaptists of his time. This asserts in general that the unimmersed are already Christians, therefore they need no other baptism than they have already received; and union can be achieved by all Christians simply recognizing this fact. The argument here is that the "one baptism" (Eph. 4:5) has been received, and is not to be repeated. Barth writes as follows:

[11] *Ibid.*, 1837, p. 414.

"Baptism without the willingness and readiness of the baptized is true, effectual, and effective baptism but it is not correct. It is not done in obedience and it is not administered according to proper order and therefore it is necessarily clouded baptism. It must and ought not to be repeated."[12]

This position (which represents fairly that of many pedobaptists of our time) does not fall far short of making baptism an *opus operatum.* If the legalistic attitudes of rigorous immersionists would hold every person, no matter his faith and character, outside God's grace until he submits to immersion, this view would bring helpless infants into the Church as the recipients of forgiveness before sins have been committed, and without the exercise of faith. Both views leave much to be desired. Ultimately the question of uniting, in one church, those who practice infant baptism with those who practice only adult baptism rests upon the conception of the nature of the church and how it is constituted. Is faith a necessary prerequisite to membership in the church? The proponents of infant baptism hold that faith (at least as exercised by the one baptized) is not necessary. As the Oberlin report phrased it, "The question of the Church has precedence over the question of baptism." To advocate the receiving of the unimmersed as a gesture of unity leaves the basic problems unsolved and may foreclose the possibility of attacking them. Some of these problems are the relation of the form of an ordinance to its meaning; the relation of faith to baptism; and the fundamental issue of church membership without a profession of faith.

The position of Alexander Campbell was somewhere between the two which we have stated. Unlike the rigorous immersionists, he did not "un-Christianize" or "unchurch" the unimmersed. Unlike the Pedobaptists, he did not advocate the attempt at union without immersion. He said in effect, "The unimmersed

[12]Barth, *op. cit.,* p. 40.

are Christians; *therefore*, they ought to be immersed, as a means of union." Writing on this topic in 1837, he said,

> . . . As every sect agrees, that a person immersed on a confession of his faith is truly baptized, and only a part of Christendom admits the possibility of any other action as baptism: for the sake of union among Christians, it may be easily shown to be the duty of all believers to be immersed . . . ; only a part of Christendom will acknowledge the sprinkled or the poured.[13]

In this argument, Campbell was going beyond his stated theory of the purpose of baptism. He had held that, in the New Testament, baptism was for the forgiveness of sins, and it was on this basis that he taught baptism for those professing faith. But baptism, in the scene of the modern divided Christian world, also has another significance: its practice bears on unity as well. Campbell also taught this.

Campbell's theory and practice of baptism are not the last word, of course, either for those who stand in his succession or for others. But it is a strong position, logically and consistently argued out. We may summarize it in our own words this way: those who are Christians without immersion and those who are Christians with immersion should unite simply because they are Christians and it is the will of Christ that they should do so. So far as baptism is concerned, all Christians can unite by submitting to that form which all Christians already acknowledge. That form is immersion in water following a profession of faith.

Campbell's position does not drive Christians out of the church. It is a positive, scripturally supported position. It will bear careful reassessment in the light of present trends toward unity.

---

[13]*Millennial Harbinger*, 1837, p. 564.

Alexander Campbell and the Social Order

Roland Bainton

Titus Street Professor of Ecclesiastical History at Yale University and author of **The Church of Our Fathers**

Alexander Campbell in his social outlook was a highly representative American of the first half of the nineteenth century. He combined all of the dominant attitudes of the time, many of them disparate in origin and incongruous at least in their implications. Somehow he managed to hold them all together and to arrive at a conclusion which added up about to this: that society is riddled by evils, that these evils are capable of redress, and that America offers a better opportunity than anywhere else in the world for their elimination. In this land, by the effort of man and the grace of God, the millennium will shortly be introduced.

Into this amalgam went some surprising ingredients. Alexander Campbell was a Bible Christian, a Protestant of the left, a sectarian who believed in the separation of Church and State because the Church might be sullied through association with an agency of this present evil world. Nevertheless, at the same time he endorsed without qualm the views of Jefferson stemming from the Enlightenment, who desired the separation of Church and State lest the State be subject to clericalism, who demanded universal suffrage, universal education, and proclaimed the fundamental and universal rights of man. Campbell was tinged by the Romantic Movement which looked upon nature as relucent with God, and regarded the American wilderness as that free environment in which the soul of man would not be stifled. Yet he recorded with pride America's material progress and enormous increase in population. He shared with the puritans the belief in the possibility of a Holy Commonwealth and merged this ideal, as did many of them in the eighteenth century, with the thousand-year reign of prosperity and peace which should precede the coming of the Messiah. Thus left-wing Protestantism, the rationalism of the Enlightenment, Romanticism, Puritan Theocracy, and Millenarinism formed a fluctuating and yet fairly stable union.

Let us begin by examining his view of nature and of America. Campbell shared with the Romantics of his generation the view of nature as the garment of God. He has a rhapsodic passage on sunrise at sea, couched in a diction too florid for the taste of our generation.[1] Somewhat more restrained, though no less vibrant, is the report of his biographer on his feelings as he first contemplated the American forest.

In the exaltation of his youthful feelings he seemed to have reached a land of enchantment. The moon, already high in heaven

[1]Richardson, *op. cit.*, II, pp. 419-20.

and nearly at the full, seemed to mingle its silvery beams with the sun's golden radiance reflected from the western sky. The mighty trees, in all their wild luxuriance, stood around him, forming aloft, as it were, a new heaven of verdure; while, beneath, he trod upon the soil of a new world—the land of liberty and of Washington, whose liberal institutions had long been the object of his admiration. All nature around him seemed to sympathize with his emotions. The balmy air, fresh from the wild mountain slopes, the new varieties of birds, which from almost every tree seemed, to his fancy, to chant their evening song in praise of the freedom of their native woods, the approaching shades of evening, veiling the distant landscape in a gentle haze—all seemed to speak of liberty, security and peace. . . . Keenly susceptible as he was to impressions of grandeur, and tending still, in the habitual workings of his mind, to religious thought, as he ranged through the deep, untrodden glades, or paused beneath the canopy of verdure which the wild vine had woven as the woof upon the spreading warp of branching oaks, his heart overflowed with gratitude and reverence.[2]

Alexander Campbell took care, however, to seal off his Romanticism in such fashion that it compromised in no sense his biblical faith. There is no such thing, said he, as natural religion. God illumines nature, but nature does not reveal God. Without revelation we cannot so much as arrive at his existence. For that reason there cannot be a rational Deist, for whatever he believes in the way of religion is derived precisely from that revelation which he rejects.

But when it came to the cult of America, Campbell was not so successful in compartmentalizing. His view was a blend of cultural primitivism, the idea of progress, the ideal of the Holy Commonwealth, a sense of national mission, and the expectation of Christ's kingdom. The cultural primitivism centered not on the *bon sauvage,* the American Indian, but on the sturdy frontiersman. We see him

moccasined with his deer-skin boots, wrapped in his hunting-shirt, with a tomahawk suspended from his girdle on his right side, and

[2] *Ibid.,* I, p. 207.

a scalping-knife, sheathed in a deer-skin scabbard, dangling on his left, with rifle on his shoulder, his faithful dog by his side, [as he] sallies forth from his cabin or his fort, at early dawn, and, with cautious step and listening ear, surveys his environs. If neither man nor savage beast greets his watchful eye, he grounds his rifle, seizes his axe, and begins to girdle the forest-tree, or, with mattock in hand, engages in grubbing the virgin earth in quest of his daily bread. Gathering courage as he proceeds, day after day the forests bow beneath his sturdy strokes, and an opening is made through which the sun penetrates the newly-opened soil and quickens into life the precious seeds which, with so much parsimony, he had hopefully deposited in the bosom of his mother earth. Thus began, twice forty years ago, the settlements around us.[3]

At this juncture one might have expected Campbell to have interjected perhaps a lament over the passing of the forest primeval. There were Americans during this period who bemoaned "the primordial hills shorn of their locks." Campbell was not of their number. He goes on to exult in the march of civilization.

On every side around us, far as the eye can reach, a thousand hills and valleys, waving in rich harvests or covered with green pastures, overspread with bleating flocks of sheep or lowing herds of cattle, interspersed with beautiful villas and romantic hamlets, shaded with venerable oaks, the remains of ancient forests, or enclosed with evergreens of other climes, that vie with each other in lending enchantment to the scenes that environ the homesteads of the rugged pioneers of the great and mighty West, present themselves to our enraptured vision . . . .

And what shall we say of the sons and daughters of those brave and magnanimous pioneers? We are unable to do them justice. The beautiful towns and cities spread all over the new western world, "with glistening spires and pinnacles adorned," pyramidal trophies of industrial art, monuments of generous liberality, piety and good sense, in solemn and majestic silence, speak their praise.[4]

---

[3]*Popular Lectures and Addresses* (Cincinnati, 1863), p. 175
[4]*Ibid.*, pp. 175-76.

On another occasion he lauded the amazing resources of the land, the astounding growth in population at a rate which might bring the total to 7,000,000 within the lifetime of some there present. He spoke of the great increase in commerce without and within, for "the Father of Waters with his unnumbered tributaries" bore to New Orleans the gleanings of shores twelve thousand miles in extent. "Already we travel on canals more than four thousand miles, and on railroads over five thousand, and in this land we have four thousand four hundred and eighty-eight post offices!"[5]

In both of these addresses he breaks off at this point to extol America's spiritual greatness. The greatness of America, declared Campbell, lay in her system of universal education, including women as well as men, in her defense of human rights, and here he inserted praise for Jefferson whose name will descend "to the latest generation in that halo of glory which encircled the sun of our destiny on the first morn of its rising."[6] How different from the attitude of the New England Congregationalists to Jefferson! Our land, said Campbell, is peculiarly blessed because peopled by Anglo-Saxons to whom God has given the scepter of Judah and by Protestants, for Catholicism had made France into a nation of infidels. The very heart of popedom is gangrenous. America enjoys also the separation of Church and State. All of these astounding advantages have given to her a singular opportunity and a unique mission. Let her perceive the hour of her destiny; *kairon gnoothi,* for all his scorn of sophistication Campbell did not disdain to quote Greek. This is the *kairos* of America.[7]

Naturally, American utopianism with its secular strain could easily be combined with Christian millenarianism. The millennium, said Campbell,

[5]*Ibid.,* pp. 495-96.
[6]*Ibid.,* p. 181.
[7]"Address on the Destiny of Our Country," *Popular Lectures,* 1852.

will be a state of greatly enlarged and continuous prosperity, in which the Lord will be exalted and his divine spirit enjoyed in an unprecedented measure. All the conditions of society will be vastly improved; wars shall cease, and peace and good will among men will generally abound. . . . Genuine Christianity will be diffused through all nations; crimes and punishments will cease; governments will recognize human rights, and will rest on just and benevolent principles . . . [There will be] one extended and protracted series of revivals . . . [and even] the seasons will become more mild; climates more salubrious, health more vigorous, labor less, lands more fertile, and the animal creation more prolific.[8]

At the same time Campbell was a vigorous critic of his culture and his land. One would expect this in a descendant of Protestant sectaries, congenital Elijahs immolating the priests of Baal. Harold Lunger has called attention to the fluctuations in Campbell's rhapsodies over America. He was disillusioned by Georgia's violation of the rights of the Cherokee Indians, Virginia's dilatoriness in taking any action to alleviate the lot of the slave. The Jacksonian Spoils System betokened political degeneration, and one of the "antedeluvian signs of the times was that 'the earth was filled with violence.' " Yet he remained always an activist who believed that something could be done about it.

One agency to that end is the State, to which he accorded a somewhat grudging acquiescence. He was strongly persuaded of the separation of Church and State and the absolute inadmissability of any tampering with religion on the part of the State. Equally was he clear that the kirk is not to give laws to Caesar. He verged, at times, almost on the old Anabaptist view that the State is ordained of God because of sin and should be run by sinners. "Would to God that [Christians] would set their affection on the politics of heaven, and leave the politics of earth to those who cannot soar above the Allegheny Mountains." Nevertheless, on important issues the Christian might vote, and Campbell himself was willing to be a delegate to the Virginia Con-

[8] *Millennial Harbinger,* 1841, p. 9.

stitutional Convention of 1829-30, because the making of a fundamental political framework was of greater significance than the choice between candidates equally undesirable. And he was willing to accord to government certain of the functions in the economic sphere which we associate with the welfare state.[9] In general, his attitude *vis à vis* the State grew less intransigent with the years.

He never ceased to regard the church as the primary sphere for Christian activity, and that was why he so sharply disapproved of societies. One might have expected him to be cordial because they originated in part to obviate that very denominationalism which he deplored. Men of all religious persuasions or of none were invited to unite on a single point of agreement and endeavor. There was a society to emancipate Negroes, a society to educate Negroes, a society to repatriate Negroes. In such a project to send the Negroes back to Africa co-operation could be enlisted from Baptists, Methodists, Presbyterians, Catholics, and infidels. But that was just the trouble, in Campbell's eyes. Alliances were being made with the sons of Ashdod, and in any case membership in a society of whatever sort was a diversion of interest and effort from the church. In later life he relaxed at the point of missionary societies and slightly as to temperance.[10] But he was never of the view that the Church herself should espouse social reforms after the manner of societies; rather her task was to make Christian citizens.

As a Christian citizen Campbell was active in sponsoring many social reforms. The two chief reforms were antislavery and war. His views on slavery have been so well delineated by Lunger that I may content myself with a summary and a comparison with the position of some New Englanders in the same period.

Campbell was thoroughly convinced that the slave trade is evil and blazed out against those who would raid the African

[9]See Lunger, *op. cit.*, pp. 191-92.
[10]*Ibid.*, pp. 44-48.

coast and separate families. But he did not feel that the holding of slaves is of itself wrong, if their treatment be humane. The primary ground for this position was biblical. Neither the Old Testament nor the New Testament forbids slave-holding. On this point Campbell was unquestionably right. He held further that slavery in the United States was not worse than in the days of the Apostle Paul. That assumption is almost certainly wrong, because the word used by Paul for *slave* is often so mild in meaning that in English it is better rendered simply by the word *servant*. On the basis of these assumptions Campbell could not be persuaded to stigmatize slave-holding as necessarily a sin.

Of couse it might be a sin, and he heartily concurred in the action of his father who had moved out of the state of Kentucky because of interference with his activities in instructing Negroes. To hold them in servitude and to keep them illiterate was indeed a sin. Moreover, Alexander Campbell held that although slave-holding might not be a sin, yet slavery was inexpedient and should as speedily as possible be abolished. The arguments which he used referred mainly to the deleterious effects upon the white population rather than to the injustice to the Negroes. Servile governesses were not the best guides to the youth of a free people. Slave insurrections kept the master in continual fear of his property and life. More important even than the emancipation of the slave was the emancipation of the master. Economically the system of slavery was unproductive and would be the very ruin of Virginia.

Some strictures have been leveled against Campbell at this point because he burned with concern for the self-interest of the white rather than blazed with indignation against the oppression of the black. The criticism is not altogether unjustified, but one must not forget that in his own mind this was an instance in which Christian and non-Christian motives converged, and he may have felt that his plea would be more heeded if based on grounds appealing to the entire populace and not merely to churchmen.

Several courses of action commended themselves as feasible. The first was private emancipation and this course Campbell took himself until he came to have no slaves. The second was a gradual emancipation to be undertaken by the government. Campbell did not favor emancipation without indemnification because the slave is property. He would devote federal funds to the reimbursement of owners and then to the colonization of the emancipated slaves in Africa. This was the great scheme of colonization which for several decades was the method most approved by many of the South and also of the North. Another way was the system of gradual emancipation. In 1849 Campbell gave support to a plan proposed by Henry Clay whereby all slaves born after 1855 or 1860 should be free on attaining the age of twenty-five.[11] This was the system by which slavery had been terminated in Connecticut, so that by 1850 there was not a slave remaining.

Thus far Campbell's position was entirely in accord with that of the Northern moderates. I have been studying lately the position taken by the Yale circle and such men as Nathaniel W. Taylor, Leonard Bacon, and Moses Stuart. These men also held that slave-holding is not as such a sin. Stuart, who was a great biblical scholar, stoutly maintained like Campbell that the New Testament has no more by way of prohibition than the Old Testament. Taylor considered *Uncle Tom's Cabin* a gross exaggeration, and Leonard Bacon, when asked whether he would receive to his pulpit a slave-holding Presbyterian minister from the South, said that he would not admit him simply because he was a Presbyterian nor reject him simply because he was a slave-holder, but would inquire why. Attention was called by these Northerners to the dilemma of the Southern Christian who had inherited slaves, who treated them humanely, who would like to

---

[11]Campbell's position on slavery is well set forth by Lunger.

set them free but feared to do so lest in a hostile society they should find nowhere to lay their heads. George Park Fisher of the Divinity School declared that to tell the South to liberate all the slaves at once was like telling an eagle in midair with a lamb in its talons to let go before coming down. These Northerners were all in favor of gradualism. They, too, endorsed and strenuously fostered the colonization plan, but the trouble here was that after fifteen years the number of Negroes transported to Africa did not equal the natural increase in the United States. The Abolitionists, therefore, began to stigmatize the plan as a diversion. They rejected it also for precisely the reason which commended it to the moderates; namely, that southern slaveholders would co-operate. Anything in which they would join, said the abolitionists, must be wrong because slave-holding is *sin.* Campbell countered by saying that abolitionism is sin because of its intolerant spirit and unbiblical basis.

Colonization was, as a matter of fact, so unfeasible that by 1840 it had been dropped in the North. Campbell continued to advocate it as late as 1850. But in the meantime a much more serious question had arisen as to whether the Fugitive Slave Law should be obeyed. The North was seriously divided at this point. There were some like Daniel Webster and Moses Stuart who counseled obedience. So also did Alexander Campbell, and of course the South in general. The reasons adduced were different. The argument in the North was not merely that obedience would preserve the Union but also that obedience was a path to the ultimate emancipation of the slaves as a whole. It was pointed out that there were only two ways in which the slaves in the South could be freed. One was by persuasion of the owners; the other was by force. But that would mean war. There was, to be sure, a third course open, namely, the disruption of the Union and secession. This would save the North from pollution, but would not emancipate the slaves in the South. The best method then would be to preserve the Union and induce the South to take voluntary action. To that end property rights would have to be respected and fugitive slaves returned. Any other course would end in secession or war or both.

Campbell appears not to have defended compliance as requisite for mass emancipation but rather on the ground that disobedience would disrupt the churches and the nation. He had a frightful dread of division in the churches. The Methodists, the Presbyterians, and the Baptists were splitting over the issue. He would take no position which would cause Disciples of Christ also to divide. His church unity program, in other words, made him less sensitive to the claims of justice. The other concern was for peace. He was aghast at those who were resolved that the matter

> shall only be discussed by the light of burning palaces, cities, and temples, amidst the roar of cannon, the clangor of trumpets, the shrieks of dying myriads. . . . the horrid din and crash of a broken confederacy . . . and the agonizing throes of the last and best republics on earth![12]

So also in the North, Leonard Bacon only a few weeks prior to the attack on Fort Sumter felt that secession was to be preferred.

Since we know only too well the outcome we may pass over to Campbell's views on war. He was not an extremist and did not reject even capital punishment, because it is inflicted upon the guilty. The difficulty with war is that it includes in its penalties the innocent. Much of his critique is of the sort which one finds today among Catholic conscientious objectors, who so long as they are Catholic cannot deny the legitimacy of the just war, but deny that any modern war can satisfy the conditions. Campbell was more radical in that for him no war ever did or ever could meet the demand that only the guilty should be made to suffer.

The considerations which he adduced were a blend of a strict New Testament literalism resting on the Sermon on the Mount

---

[12]*Millennial Harbinger,* 1835, p. 587.

and the rationalism of the Enlightenment, which deemed it more prudent to obtain peace by purchase than to have recourse to war. Witness the policy of the great Jefferson in the Louisiana Purchase. War is contrary, said Campbell, to the spirit of Jesus. War is unbefitting men endowed with reason and sense. War is destructive of property, devastating of life, and debauching to morals. Lunger has well summarized Campbell's main arguments in his *Address on War* where it is urged that "war is *folly,* because 'it can never be a satisfactory end of the controversy,' and 'peace is always the result of negotiations.' " Campbell argued further the wickedness of war "on the rational and pragmatic grounds that 'those who are engaged in killing their brethren, for the most part, have no personal cause of provocation whatever;' 'they seldom . . . comprehend the right or the wrong of the war' and act therefore 'without the approbation of conscience;' 'the innocent are punished with the guilty;' the soldier is constrained 'to do for the state that, which, were he to do in his own case, the state would condemn him to death;' and wars 'are the pioneers of all other evils to society, both moral and physical.' "

One can disparage, if one will, the pacifism of Alexander Campbell on the grounds that it was only the mood of the moment. One cannot deny, of course, that he lived in the period when first opposition to war took hold of the American mind, except, of course, the traditional peace churches—the Quakers, the Mennonites, and the Brethren. Notably the Congregationalists and the Presbyterians had been far removed from pacifism and had looked upon the French and Indian War and the Revolutionary War as crusades. There were, to be sure, Tories in New England but they were primarily Episcopalians who objected to resistance to the Lord's anointed. The first revulsion against war came after the conflict of 1812 which had been highly unpopular on the Atlantic seaboard. The formation of the American Peace Society, by which Campbell was so much influenced (even if it was a society), occurred in 1815. The Mexican War received general disapprobation in New England and Campbell heartily concurred. He was not as remote as New England but still not near enough to the Rio Grande to be going against the current of popular opinion by his opposition. The great test was the Civil War. He was an old man then and, in the words of a friend, in almost imperceptible decay. His writing grew diffuse and rambling. But the question of war so affected him that he rallied into lucidity and in 1861 made this statement in the *Millennial Harbinger:*

> Of all the monstrosities on which our sun has ever shone, that of professedly *Christian* nations, glutting their wrath and vengeance on one another, with all the instruments of murder and slaughter, caps the climax of human folly and gratuitous wickedness. Alas! Alas! man's inhumanity to man has made, and is still intent on making, countless millions mourn![13]

---

[13] *Ibid.*, 1861, pp. 345-48.

Alexander Campbell Against Socialism

PERRY EPLER GRESHAM

President of Bethany College and author of **Disciplines of the High Calling**

Alexander Campbell, founder of Bethany College, deserves an honorable place in American history as an exponent of free enterprise and an ardent foe of socialism. When Robert Owen undertook the socialization of America by means of pamphleteering, a lecture tour, and the establishment of a communistic community at New Harmony, Indiana, it was Campbell who met him in debate at Cincinnati and reduced his great prestige before the public. Ohio was a stronghold for Owenism in the third decade of the nineteenth century. A community designed along the lines of his socialism was established at Kendall in

Stark County. One Dr. Underhill was creating such concern in Canton that an acquaintance of Campbell wrote asking him to come to Canton and debate the socialist who was "indefatigably engaged in preaching that sort of moral philosophy which the New Harmony Gazette contains." Campbell declined, but indicated his willingness to meet Robert Owen himself. His exact words were that he "would not draw a bow save at the king of sceptics of the city of mental independence."

Without Campbell's knowledge Owen was already asking for debate. In January, 1828, the city of New Orleans heard Robert Owen fling down the challenge to all leaders of religion without a response. Campbell printed the challenge and his answer to it in the *Christian Baptist* of August 4, 1828:

A Debate on the Evidence of Christianity

It will be remembered that Mr. Robert Owen, of New Harmony, did, in the month of January last, challenge the clergy of New Orleans (as he had in effect the teachers of religion every where) to debate with him the truth of the christian religion. In his public discourses, as well as in the words of that challenge, he engages to prove that *"all the religions of the world have been founded on the ignorance of mankind; that they have been, and are, the real sources of vice, disunion, and misery of every description; that they are now the only bar to the formation of a society of virtue, of intelligence, of charity in its most extended sense, and of sincerity and kindness among the whole human family; and that they can be no longer maintained except through the ignorance of the mass of the people, and the tyranny of the few over that mass."* This challenge I have formally accepted, believing it to be my duty so to do in existing circumstances; and I stand pledged to prove, in a public discussion, that the above positions are every one untenable; that Mr. Owen *cannot* prove any one of them by any fair or legitimate process of reasoning whatsoever."[1]

[1]*The Christian Baptist,* II, p. 469.

Mr. Owen called at Bethany to discuss the forthcoming verbal battle with Alexander Campbell. Richardson reports that the British philosopher was "greatly delighted with the beautiful hills and landscapes to which Mr. Campbell called his attention during their pleasant walks in the vicinity of Bethany."[2]

The debate was set for Cincinnati on the second Monday in April, 1829. This date was to coincide with Mr. Owens' return from England. Campbell proceeded to marry a new wife, lecture throughout the nation, publish his monthly journal and tend the sheep on his vast Virginia farm. Owen departed for England to return armed for the intellectual combat.

The debate came off as scheduled on April 13, 1829, at a large Methodist Church in Cincinnati. Owen was to open at nine o'clock in the morning of the first day with a thirty-minute address after which Campbell was to have equal time. The debate was to continue until "the parties agree to adjourn." It lasted through Tuesday, April 21, with time out for the Lord's Day when Campbell preached to a vast audience just to keep in practice. The sessions ran from nine to twelve and from three until dark. The moderators were "Judge Burnet, Major Daniel Gano, Col. Francis Carr, the Rev. Timothy Flint, the Rev. Oliver Spencer, Henry Starr, Esq. and Col. Samuel W. Davis." Campbell had the closing address.

Robert Owen was fifty-eight years of age when he arose and began in a calm clear voice, "Gentlemen Moderators." His first few sentences placed his central conviction before the audience. He said, "All societies of men have been formed on a misapprehension of the primary laws of human nature." He continued with a bill of particulars which outlined his central views on man, society, and religion.

1. That man, at his birth, is ignorant of every thing relative to his own organization, and that he has not been permitted to create

---

[2]Richardson, *op. cit.*, II, p. 242.

the slightest part of his natural propensities, faculties, or qualities, physical or mental.

2. That no two infants, at birth, have yet been known to possess precisely the same organization, while the physical, mental, and moral differences, between all infants, are formed without their knowledge or will.

3. That each individual is placed, at birth, without his knowledge or consent, within circumstances, which, acting upon his peculiar organization, impress the general character of those circumstances upon the infant, child, and man. Yet that the influence of these circumstances is to a certain degree modified by the peculiar natural organization of each individual.

4. That no infant has the power of deciding at what period of time or in what part of the world he shall come into existence; of whom he shall be born, in what distinct religion he shall be trained to believe, or by what other circumstances he shall be surrounded from birth to death.

5. That each individual is so created, that when young, he may be made to receive impressions, to produce either true ideas or false notions, and beneficial or injurious habits, and to retain them with great tenacity.

6. That each individual is so created, that he must believe according to the strongest impressions that are made on his feelings and other faculties, while his belief in no case depends upon his will.

7. That each individual is so created that he must like that which is pleasant to him, or that which produces agreeable sensations on his individual organization, and he must dislike that which creates in him unpleasant and disagreeable sensations; while he cannot discover, previous to experience, what those sensations should be.

8. That each individual is so created, that the sensations made upon his organization, although pleasant and delightful at their commencement and for some duration, generally become, when continued beyond a certain period, without change, disagreeable and painful; while, on the contrary when a too rapid change of sensations is made on his organization, it dissipates, weakens, and otherwise injures his physical, intellectual, and moral powers and enjoyments.

9. That the highest health, the greatest progressive improvements, and the most permanent happiness of each individual de-

pend, in a great degree, upon the proper cultivation of all his physical, intellectual and moral faculties and powers from infancy to maturity, and upon all these parts of his nature being duly called into action, at their proper period, and temperately exercised according to the strength and capacity of the individual.

10. That the individual is made to possess and to acquire the *worst* character, when his organization at birth has been compounded of the most inferior propensities, faculties and qualities of our common nature, and when so organized, he has been placed, from birth to death, amid the most vicious or worst circumstances.

11. That the individual is made to possess and to acquire a *medium* character, when his original organization has been created *superior*, and when the circumstances which surround him from birth to death produce continued *vicious* or *unfavorable* impressions. Or when his organization has been formed of *inferior* materials, and the circumstances in which he has been placed, from birth to death, are of a character to produce *superior* impressions only. Or when there has been some mixture of *good* and *bad* qualities, in the original organization, and when it has been also placed, through life, in various circumstances of *good* and *evil*. This last compound has been hitherto the common lot of mankind.

12. That the individual is made the most *superior* of his species when his original organization has been compounded of the best proportions of the best ingredients of which human nature is formed, and when the circumstances which surround him from birth to death are of a character to produce only *superior* impressions; or, in other words, when the circumstances or laws, institutions, and customs, in which he is placed, are all in unison with his nature.[3]

His twelve laws of nature revealed a philosophical determination which denied any free choice or action to any man. Freedom of the will was to him an utter delusion. Since man is completely the product of his environment he can be controlled by education in a comprehensive context. His schools and communities were efforts at providing optimum conditions to form perfect people. "No praise; no blame" was his maxim since man is a creature

[3]*Evidences of Christianity.* Owen and Campbell, pp. 22-24.

of his environment and not responsible for his beliefs, actions, and decisions. He took a loose view of marriage, and urged that children should be reared by nurses rather than by their parents. Private property was to be abolished. Religion, as an inherited superstition, was to be utterly obliterated. It is interesting to note that the term "socialism" first became current in "The Association of All Classes and Nations" which Owen formed in 1835.

Owen brought with him an international reputation as a genius at management of the New Lanark Mills, the founder of the infant school in that city, a political philosopher, and a completely unselfish philanthropist. Such a person was not to be brushed aside as crank or fanatic. Governments were disposed to listen to him. Lord Liverpool had called him for interview and Nicholas, later Emperor of Russia, had visited his New Lanark factory and school. In 1813 Owen had published *A New View of Society* which had created a considerable stir among the intellectuals. He had commanded world attention by his proposals for the cure of pauperism. His ambitious scheme for social amelioration was to include community after community until the entire world was encompassed.

Campbell arose when Owen yielded the floor. He was tall and impressive at the ascendency of his career as a preacher, educator, farmer, and publisher. His forty years had been almost equally divided between Ireland and America. His natural eloquence, his thorough mind and his argumentative nature, had seasoned him for debate. After the first prepared address designed to outline some evidences of Christianity he proceeded extemporaneously. He tried to keep the conversation centered on the antireligious sentiments of Owen's thought, since this was the subject of the challenge, as well as Campbell's greatest competence. His shrewd insight into public opinion told him that here Owen was most vulnerable. Campbell was a systematic thinker. He was fully aware of the fact that religion is the most fundamental enemy of every utopian scheme which aims at the destruction of such fundamental social institutions as marriage, private property, and individual responsibility.

As the debate continued, the casual auditor gained the impression that the speakers were expounding separate views without a genuine encounter. The more thoughtful members of the 1,200 Americans in attendance, however, saw the issues joined as early as Tuesday, which was only the second of the eight days of battle. Owen had set forth five of his twelve points with sufficient clarity that his political and social views of determinism, irresponsibility, and religious skepticism were apparent. Campbell countered with

> If I could be brought to admit that man is altogether a material being, a pure animal, I could have little difficulty in admitting the whole of Mr. Owen's theory. I could then be brought to believe that all our ideas of our natural, moral, social and religious relations, obligations and dependencies were absurd. I earnestly wish that my friend was more fully aware, than he seems to be, that while he is thus aiming at the extermination of all bad feelings, he is in reality sapping the foundations of society.[4]

He continued to discredit the system with

> We say that infants, idiots, lunatics, and the *non compos mentis,* are irresponsible, and we have guardians assigned them. All societies agree that these are irresponsible, because they are either untaught, or unteachable. But carry out Mr. Owen's principles to their legitimate length, and the conclusion irresistibly follows that all men are reduced to the state of *non compos mentis*—the sage is as irresponsible as the idiot. Irrational animals and vegetables are to be loved or hated, praised or dispraised—are as sociable, as responsible and as irresponsible as philosphers. There can be no responsibility exacted from any human being on these principles, more than from a stone, a tree, a horse, or a dog.[5]

---

[4]*Ibid.,* pp. 50-60.
[5]*Ibid.,* pp. 60-61.

The older man did not strike back at the charge. He preferred, rather, to continue expounding his twelve laws of human nature as the panacea for human ills and unhappiness. He praised his system with a confident extravagance:

There never was, in the imagination of any human being, a collection of facts so truly valuable to the whole of mankind as those which are contained in these twelve laws; each one of them is of invaluable truth. But when united and formed into a system for reforming the character of men and governing them, what a glorious change will be effected for the well-being and happiness of the human race? When this shall be accomplished, as I anticipate will be the case in a few years, how very different will our residence in this world become?[6]

As Owen reiterated and expounded his twelve laws of human nature Campbell continued to attack first, the doctrine of environmental determinism which was later to appear in Marxism as economic determinism, and second, the derived doctrine of no responsibility. By Monday afternoon of the second week Campbell was ready to deal some sledge-hammer blows.

No social compact has as yet existed, without the doctrine of responsibility, obligation, or accountability. Mr. Owen's scheme is the most Utopian project in the annals of society. He lays the ax at the root of all obligation and accountability, and yet would have society to hang together without a single attraction, save animal magnetism, if such a thing exist. The doctrine of *no praise, no blame,* is to be taught from the cradle to the grave; and yet all are to live in accordance with the most virtuous principles. They are to have no principle of responsibility suggested; and yet under the charm of social feeling alone, they are to be more firmly bound than any wedded pair! Among the visions of the wildest enthusiasm, this one appears to be a rarity.

Children are to be reared without a lesson upon obligation or duty, and yet they are to be most orderly, neither selfish, querulous, peevish, ambitious, nor in any way vicious. All these evil propensities are to be eradicated from their nature in consequence of being

[6] *Ibid.*, p. 70.

born in chambers, ventilated, heated, or refrigerated, in the social way. They are to be models of beauty and rationality, too, by a mere change of circumstances. No irrational faces, no deformed countenances, no disfigured frames can grow in any of Mr. Owen's parallelogram arrangements. The romantic genius of Mr. Owen gives these babes all angelic charms, excepting wings; and while there is to be a total destitution of evil disposition, they are to be perfect giants in literature, virtue, and benevolent enterprise—able in two hours per diem, to provide for all their own happiness and to perpetuate overflowing streams of bliss to posterity!

I am yet at a loss to know what Mr. Owen means by *society*. A society without a social compact, to me is unintelligible. Society is not a number of persons covering a certain piece of ground, like the trees in our forests. They must congregate upon some stipulations, expressed or implied. These stipulations are to be performed, and consequently, responsibility or accountability forces itself upon Mr. Owen in defiance of the powers of his imagination. In all other societies, except Mr. Owen's imaginary one, the people and the magistracy, whether elective or hereditary, are mutually accountable to each other. The people owe *allegiance*, which they promise in electing their rulers; and the magistracy owe *protection* which they promise in being elected. In entering into society man surrenders a part of his natural liberty for other benefits, which he could not enjoy as a hermit. This surrender he must never recall, nor those benefits must they withhold; they are, therefore, under continual obligations to each other. Whenever any person feels himself absolved from these obligations, he is either dangerous to, or unfit for, society. And certainly Mr. Owen's system of training children would naturally lead them to feel themselves absolved from all such obligations. His system directly unfits them for society. I would ask you, my friends, or I would ask him, in what light he could contemplate that society which taught every child that entered its schools, that the child which would kill its own father was not to be blamed or disliked any more than the child which loved, caressed and reverenced its father?[7]

From this position Campbell moved on to set forth his views of Christian social amelioration which was to be accomplished

[7] *Ibid.*, pp. 392-93.

on the basis of better men for better times. When the love and power of God lay hold of a man so that he can hunger for truth and walk in humility and brotherhood with his fellows, the good society can emerge. Individual Christian responsibility was the center of Campbell's approach to a righteous social order. This brought fire from Owen.

A christian population is, emphatically, in practice, a population preying upon each other, and living very generally in a state of unnatural anxiety, for useless and surplus property, in the midst of hourly deception and hypocrisy; hating and disliking each other because they cannot think and feel alike, having been taught the notion that they may think and feel as they please. It is everywhere a population of inequality of condition, and necessarily, of pride, poverty, envy, and jealousy. It is a population in which tenfold more of exertion and anxiety is required from each, to produce the misery they experience, than is necessary to secure a full supply of the best of every thing for all. In short, I find it to be, in practice, so full of ignorance, weakness, insincerity, and counteraction of each other's views and objects, and of weekly preaching to perpetuate all these evils, that did I not firmly believe that truth is omnipotent to remove error, and that we are, in consequence, rapidly approaching a new state of existence, in which, with regard to these things, there will be a new birth and a new life, a regeneration that will purge man from all these abominations, I could feel no interest in the present irrational proceedings of the human race. And if I had wanted any further proof of the christian world being in this wretched condition, Mr. Campbell's sermon in this place on Sunday last, and the appearance of the state of mind of the congregation, would have rendered more unnecessary. Never did I see so much fine talent so miserably misdirected. Never did I see human beings so ready to receive poison under the undoubting supposition that it was good and wholesome food.[8]

Campbell came back with an elaboration of his individualistic religious views:

Christianity had its direct and its indirect influences upon society. The direct or the reflex light of this holy religion affects almost

[8]*Ibid.*, pp. 406-7.

every man in the region where it shines. It shines into the hearts of some, and in their lives it is reflected as from a mirror upon all around. And thus some are *christianized,* more are *moralized,* and all are, in some good degree, *civilized* by its light. A single pious man in a village is a restraint upon the wickedness and profanity of all the villagers. I have known some instances, and have heard of others, where a general deterioration of morals has followed the death or removal of a good man out of a small town or neighborhood. There is a charm, there is an indescribable influence in the genuine fruits of christianity, which, when exhibited in living christians, the most abandoned are constrained to respect. Hence an increase of genuine christians is one of the greatest national blessings—if, indeed, it be a truth that *righteousness exalteth a nation.*[9]

As the eight days of discussion became history and the sun was sinking over the adolescent city along the Ohio River, Robert Owen brought his presentation to a close by once more reiterating the twelve laws which he called "the twelve jewels." He saw an opportunity to make a telling point in regard to his sixth law.

Mr. Campbell has given you his views and reasonings upon this sixth law of our nature, but they amount to nothing. He did not take up the position which is here laid down. This position is, that each individual is so created, that he must believe according to the strongest impression that is made upon his feelings and other faculties, while his belief in no case depends upon his will. This is a clear and distinct position, and leaves no room for a metaphysical retreat.

Mr. Campbell rose and said.—There is no metaphysical subterfuge in me. I contend that I have met the position fairly. The clause I objected to is this: "That belief in no case depends upon will."

Mr. Owen.—Well, gentleman, I will bring this matter to a speedy issue. If Mr. Campbell can adduce a single instance wherein his belief depends upon his will, I will give up the whole question.

[9] *Ibid.*, p. 430.

[*Here Mr. Owen waited some time for Mr. Campbell's reply. Mr. Campbell could not then make any.*][10]

With an air of confident triumph Owen closed his remarks and sat down.

Campbell arose for the closing speech. He answered the challenge which had left him silent a few minutes earlier by relating an instance of murder in Frankfort, Kentucky, in which only the will to find the assassin brought Beauchamp to trial and conviction for the murder of Colonel Sharp. He then drew a sharp contrast between the order of life which would ensue with the triumph of Skepticism and that which would ensue with the triumph of Christianity. At that moment his dramatic instinct led him to a daring and devastating maneuver. He began his last remarks,

Before we dismiss this assembly, I beg leave to express my sensibility, my admiration of the marked and courteous attention which has been paid by this community to this discussion. I must again repeat that I have never seen any assembly convened upon any occasion which has all through exhibited the same good order, the same complaisant behavior, and the same unremitted attention. I feel indebted to, and will ever feel a high respect for, the citizens of this city, for the favorable circumstances which they have created for this debate; and especially to the gentlemen who have so politely and so patiently presided over this meeting.

But I should be wanting to you my friends, and the cause which I plead, if I should dismiss you without making to you a very important proposition. You know that this discussion is matter for the press. You know that every encomium that has been pronounced upon your exemplary behavior, will go with the report of this discussion. You will remember, too, that many indignities have been offered to your faith, to your religion, and that these reproaches and indignities have been only heard with pity and not marked with the least resentment on your part. Now I must tell you that a problem will arise in the minds of those living five hundred or a thousand miles distant, who may read this discussion, *whether*

[10] *Ibid.*, p. 433.

it was owing to a perfect apathy or indifference on your part, as to any interest you felt in the christian religion, that you bore all these insults without seeming to hear them. In fine, the question will be, *whether it was owing to the stoical indifference of fatalism, to the prevalence of infidelity; or, to the meekness and forbearance which christianity teaches, that you bore all these indignities without a single expression of disgust.* Now I desire no more than that this good and christian like deportment may be credited to the proper account. If it be owing to your concurrence in sentiment with Mr. Owen, let skepticism have the honor of it. But if owing to your belief in, or regard for, the christian religion, let the christian religion have the honor of it. These things promised, my proposition is, *that all the persons in this assembly who believe in the christian religion or who feel so much interest in it, as to wish to see it pervade the world, will please to signify it by standing up.* [An almost universal rising up.]

Here Mr. Campbell says, You will have the goodness to be seated.

Now I would further propose, *that all persons doubtful of the truth of the christian religion, or who do not believe it, and who are not friendly to its spread and prevalence over the world, will please signify it by rising up.* [THREE ARISE.]

Mr. OWEN rises.

Gentlemen Moderators—It has just occurred to me, that I had forgotten to tender my thanks to you for your presence and superintendence on this occasion, which I now beg leave to do. And I may add, I am much pleased with Mr. Campbell's little maneuver of the test, because I discover it pleases him and his friends. Truth requires no such support. [*Candles called for.*]

Mr. CAMPBELL rises.

While we are waiting for light, I will move that the thanks of this whole assembly be presented to the Board of Moderators, and put upon record.—*Nemine contradicente.*

Adjournment *sine die.*

CHARLES HOWARD SIMS, *Reporter*[11]

Owen was evidently aware of considerable loss of prestige. He returned to England to repudiate his agreement that the sole

[11] *Ibid.*, pp. 464-65.

rights to the printed record should go to Charles Howard Sims who had reported it. Owen published a volume called *Owen's View of Public Discussion* which was a slanted narrative giving Owen's opening address and excerpts from his remarks throughout the debate. Campbell countered by publishing the full account with an appendix by Mr. Owen and an appendix of his own. Campbell felt impelled by self-defense to include a sharp review of Owen's book.

With the heat of the controversy over, Campbell, in cool reflection, offered the opinion that Owen's philanthropic impulses might derive from vanity rather than the love of man. He wrote,

> . . . Yet strange, surpassing strange, as it is, this singular piece of animated matter called Robert Owen, which required old Nature in her laboratory six thousand years to produce, would now teach us to rebel and become seditious against the queen of fate; and would have us claim and take the liberty from nature of forming human beings to our own mind, and of changing the powers of nature; in fact, of binding her fast in our own cords, so that we shall abolish religion, matrimony and private property; put the old queen Nature into jail at New Harmony and never let her out upon a patrole of honor, as long as grass grows and water runs.
>
> Mr. Owen is, without knowing it, or intending it, the greatest advocate of *free agency* I have ever known; for he would have the present generation to adopt such arrangements, and so to new modify the circumstances that surround them as to prevent the goddess Nature from having it in her power ever to make another religious animal, another wedding, or to use the words *mine* or *thine*. And yet the chorus of his new music is, that we have no more liberty to act, than Gibraltar has to perch itself upon the cupola of the State House of Ohio. Such a philosopher is my good natured friend Robert Owen.[12]

Back in England Robert Owen continued his influence. George Soule calls him "the man who had more to do than any other with inspiring the British Socialist movement in its early stages."

---

[12]*Ibid., A. Campbell's Appendix.*

His son, Robert Dale Owen, was a radical liberal from Indiana who, with Fanny Wright exercised considerable influence over Van Buren. Robert Dale was elected to Congress where he introduced the bill for founding the Smithsonian Institution. At home he fostered a bill for liberalizing divorce in Indiana. He carried on his father's doctrine.

Robert Owen himself continued until 1858. He died in his native town of Newtown, North Wales. The thirty years of life after the Campbell debate brought him one community failure after another. He became an ardent spiritualist toward the end. Of his social nostrums, only the co-operative movement survived. His influence in America was severely shaken by the Cincinnati episode.

Campbell left Cincinnati to continue his preaching, debating, farming, and publishing. His smashing defeat of Robert Owen can be numbered among his greatest achievements. Socialism found a more difficult market in America after 1829. Campbell proved his belief in free enterprise by leaving a substantial personal estate when he died in 1866. His body rests in the cemetery at Bethany, where he and Robert Owen laid plans for the debate.

In the perspective of more than a century of history Owen stands out as the forerunner of socialism, which found its most impressive expression in the Marxian views of economic determinism and the abolition of private property with the concomitant belief that religion is "the opiate of the people." Campbell looms as a significant educator reformer who brought his forensic skill to bear on the great social issues of his time. He stood for private property, individual responsibility, the triumph of Christianity and the improvement of man by means of education. The final vote at the Cincinnati debate may yet prove prophetic.

Alexander Campbell's Political Activity and Views

HAROLD L. LUNGER

Professor of Christian Ethics at Texas Christian University and author of **The Political Ethics of Alexander Campbell**

A picture in the New York Historical Society presents Alexander Campbell in a role which will seem strange and out of character to those who know him only as a religious reformer. The water color, by George Catlin, is a composite portrait of the Virginia Constitutional Convention of 1829-30. Here Campbell sits with some of the political "greats" of his time, including former Presidents James Madison and James Monroe; John Tyler, who was destined to become president; Chief Justice John Marshall; the Governor of the state of Virginia; two United States senators and eleven representatives in Congress;

not to mention many judges, members of the bar, and other public figures.

How does it happen that Campbell, primarily a religious leader, should be thus deeply involved in political activity?

I

This question becomes even more perplexing against the background of Campbell's views on the separation of church and state and his frequent comments on politics and politicians. Campbell is a complex, even contradictory, figure—nowhere more so than in his relation to political life.

As a left-wing Protestant, he kept what he himself called "a sharp lookout" for any clerical interference with political matters as well as any governmental infringement upon freedom of religion. In this he reflected an attitude widespread at the time. Hugh B. Grigsby, one of his colleagues, reports that Campbell's presence in the Convention caused quite a stir because of the traditional "prejudice" in Virginia "on the subject of an union of religious and political functions in the same person."

Campbell often revealed a low regard for politics as a profession. In 1831, when John T. Johnson forsook political life for the ministry, Campbell exclaimed: "Sir, in *descending* from the forum and legislative hall to proclaim a crucified Savior, you have *ascended* far above all earthly crowns." The incompatibility of the spirit of politics and that of Christianity was a theme to which he often recurred. In 1838 he wrote, "Politics are a moral pestilence. . . . Christians, keep yourselves from IDOLS!" A few months later:

> . . . I know of nothing more antipodal to the gospel than politics. . . . It is about as hard for a Christian man to please unchristian constituents, as it is for any one to serve God and Mammon. The true

politician rises by descending to cater for the lusts and passions of men.[1]

Upon another occasion Campbell warned his readers against turning "politicians" and deciding questions of state policy. "We have, as *Christians,*" he said, "little to do with such matters. Political governments, in their best form, are but mere tents for pilgrims to lodge under while on their journey to the great King and Lord of all."

The party strife in connection with the presidential campaign of 1840 he likened to "the pestilential blast from the desert." Decrying the way the "mania of President-making" had sown the "fierce demon of discord" even in the church, he went on to picture the relative unimportance of the results of such an election:

To see men who profess to be on their way to a celestial throne fighting in partizan fury about the waiter at table, in an Inn at which they have stopped for a single breakfast, is sage wisdom and sound discretion compared with the conduct of some who contend with heated zeal for four years of X in preference to four years of Y, in a period of a thousand million of ages.

With this introduction he asked:

Ought Christians to take an active part in politics—in the present politics of this country? This is a question of as easy decision as it is of great moral importance. I am decidedly of opinion that they ought not. . . .

. . . Would to God that they would set their affection on the politics of heaven, and leave the politics of earth to those who cannot soar above the Alleghany mountains.[2]

II

How is it, then, that Campbell consented to run for a seat in the Virginia Convention?

[1] *Millennial Harbinger,* 1839, p. 8.
[2] *Ibid.,* 1840, pp. 413-15.

For one thing, all of the above depreciatory remarks concerning politics *followed* his experience at the Convention. They reflect, in part, his own disillusionment at Richmond where he saw at first hand the recalcitrance of vested political interests.[3]

Yet, even at the time, Campbell had some misgivings about his course of action. These apparently grew out of his left-wing emphasis upon separation of Church and State.

Campbell ran for a seat in the convention only at the insistence of his friends and neighbors. One of these later declared that the people of his district "called him to their service with an earnestness he could not refuse."

Even then Campbell felt under necessity of justifying himself. To a friend in Ireland, he wrote that he had "no taste or longings for political matters or honors." But the making of a constitution is "not like the ordinary affairs of legislation." It is "one of the most grave and solemn of all political matters." For this reason his participation in the convention was "not incompatible with the most perfect gravity and self-respect." Campbell seems to have felt at liberty to help debate and determine the fundamental principles of government, even though he disapproved of and kept personally aloof from partisan politics.

He further explained that he consented to be elected

> "because I was desirous of laying a foundation for the abolition of slavery . . . and of gaining an influence in public estimation to give currency to my writings, and to put down some calumnies afar off that I was not in good standing in my own state."[4]

When he agreed to run for one of the four seats from his senatorial district, Campbell had been given to understand he would have no competition. When another candidate entered the race against him, Campbell arose to the occasion. Instead of remaining silent, as he had planned, he made several campaign speeches.

---

[3]*See* Lunger, *op. cit.,* pp. 130 f.
[4]Richardson, *op. cit.,* II, pp. 319 f.

His speech at Monongalia on the day of the election reveals his great ability as a popular speaker and indicates that he might have gone far in politics had he chosen this as his field of endeavor. He appealed to the peculiar economic interests of his constituents, identified himself with them as "a practical farmer, holding with his own hands the plough," and closed with a humorous illustration which played upon the interests and sympathies of his hearers.

III

At Richmond, Campbell gave a good account of himself. In the Catlin painting he sits in the back row on the right as one faces the picture. But he took a back seat to no one when it came to debating the weighty issues before the convention. To the majority of his fellow delegates he seemed to be well to the *left* in his views.

The convention of 1829-30 was called as a result of mounting pressures from the western part of the state. It was the fruit of "a half century of conflict between the east and the west over representation, suffrage, and abuses in the state and local governments." In his definitive study of *Sectionalism in Virginia,* Charles H. Ambler says further:

> It was a contest between an older society with its peculiar institutions [centering around slavery] and a newer society fundamentally different from the older and inadequately represented in the lawmaking bodies. It was a contest between the owners of large estates and the owners of small farms; between a population largely English and one composed of various nationalities; and between a people whose economic interests and relations were with the South and a people whose interests and relations were mainly with the North.[5]

---

[5]*Sectionalism in Virginia from 1776 to 1861,* by Charles Henry Ambler. (Chicago: University of Chicago Press, 1910), pp. 5 f.

The people of the West especially resented the restriction of voting rights to those who possessed twenty-five acres of improved land and the prevailing system which gave slave owners additional representation in the General Assembly by virtue of the slaves they possessed. In this way many of the Western citizens were effectively disfranchised while Eastern slave owners were given disproportionate power in the state government.

Campbell made three major addresses during the fifteen weeks the convention was in session. These dealt with the basis of representation, suffrage, and the county court system. He also made numerous other shorter statements, observations, objections, and motions. His votes on all the questions which came before the convention are a matter of public record. These matters have all been surveyed in detail elsewhere.[6]

Campbell proved himself a faithful follower of John Locke and his natural rights philosophy. Familiar with the political views of Locke from his student days, he had a common "universe of discourse" with American statesmen; for the writings of Locke had been the political bible of the American people from colonial times.

Campbell also faithfully reflected the liberal views which prevailed in the western part of his state. He advocated the striking out of property qualifications for voting and holding office, elimination of poll taxes, and abolition of the prevailing basis of representation. He voted for the popular election of governor and county court justices, lowering the minimum age of senators from 30 to 25, and other controversial, liberal measures.[7]

Campbell was, in short, a consistent "reformer" in the terms of Ambler's analysis of the political theories represented at the

[6]See Lunger, *op. cit.*, Chapter VI.

[7]He voted *against* a provision prohibiting ministers of the gospel from holding a seat in the General Assembly and *for* disqualifying from any public office anyone who had been a party to or challenged another to a duel. But he opposed an amendment that would have required any candidate for office to give an oath that he had not violated this provision regarding duelling.

Virginia Convention. In fact Ambler himself, on at least four occasions, quotes Campbell as a particularly effective voice of the western reformer group. Writing in 1953, William H. Gaines, Jr. refers to Campbell as one of the three "most prominent western proponents of change." This statement occurs in an article in the *Virginia Cavalcade* which accompanies a reproduction of the Catlin portrait previously mentioned.[8]

With the exception of differences on relatively minor issues, Campbell's votes at Richmond went right down the line with those of the three other delegates from his senatorial district. Although few of the liberal positions they advocated gained acceptance in 1829-30, almost all of them were adopted by the "Reform Convention" of 1850-51.

IV

In the course of the debates Campbell tangled with some of the most prominent figures in the convention, including John Marshall, John Randolph, and Judge Able P. Upsher. In these verbal battles Campbell easily held his own.

Some of his most interesting exchanges were with John Randolph, one of the most eloquent and often sarcastic of the old-school conservatives. Campbell had urged that the way to proceed with the development of a constitution was simply to interpret the plain meaning of the various articles of the Declaration of Rights. Randolph ridiculed the idea that politics is that simple. If that were the case, he said, a statesman needs not even "the four rules of arithmetic. No, Sir, a negro boy with a knife and a tally-stick is a Statesman complete in this school."[9]

---

[8]"The Evening of Their Glory," *Virginia Cavalcade,* III, No. 1 (Summer, 1953), 21. Campbell, Gaines declares, was "one of the most controversial figures in the convention," . . . "took a prominent part in debate," and "preached to large congregations every Sunday during the course of the convention."

[9]*Proceedings and Debates of the Virginia State Convention of 1829-30,* p. 317.

After Randolph had angrily protested against "his majesty *King Numbers,*" Campbell came to the defense of majority rule:

King Numbers, Mr. Chairman, is the legitimate sovereign of all this country. General Jackson . . . is only the representative, the *lawful representative* of King Numbers. And, whither, Sir, can that gentleman fly from the government of this King? . . . Except he cross the ocean, he can put himself under no other King. And whenever he may please to expatriate himself, he will find beyond the dominions of King Numbers, there is no other monarch, save King Cypher, King Blood, King Sword, or King Purse. And . . . there is none of those so august as our King. I love King Numbers; I wish to live, and I hope to die, under the government of this majestic personage. He is, Sir, a wise, benevolent, patriotic and powerful prince—the most dignified personage under the canopy of Heaven.[10]

Randolph had earlier quoted in English the first part of a Latin statement by Bacon. Campbell came back with the entire quotation in the original, turning it cleverly against his opponent. Almost a quarter of a century later one of Campbell's colleagues recalled this incident with great relish.

Campbell won the respect and admiration even of those who vigorously opposed him on basic issues.

On the way home from the convention, James Madison stopped over night at the home of Philip Pendleton. To his host, Madison expressed a high regard for Campbell's abilities in debate upon the fundamental principles of government. One version of the story has it that Mr. Pendleton asked Madison, "Mr. President, who was the greatest man at the convention?" Madison replied,

"Sir, the greatest man was Alexander Campbell, of Brooke County. His mastery of the great questions which came before us, his skill in debate, was a constant surprise. In addition I heard him

[10] *Ibid.,* p. 389.

night after night as he preached in the Sycamore meetinghouse, and as an expounder of the Scriptures, I have never heard his equal."[11]

Another member of the convention, the conservative Hugh Grigsby, said of him:

He was a fine scholar, and with the younger members of the body who relished his amusing thrusts, his pleasant address and social feelings rendered him most acceptable. As a controversialist he had some great qualities; he was bold, subtle, indefatigable, and as insensible to attack as if he were sheathed in the hide of a rhinoceros.[12]

This statement occurs in an address given before the Virginia Historical Society almost a quarter of a century later. In referring to Campbell, Grigsby departed from his original plan of dealing only with deceased members of the original body. Campbell, he said, "from his unique position, though still living, [deserves] a short notice."

It is also significant that when the Catlin picture of the Virginia Convention was reproduced in color as a two-page center spread in the *Virginia Cavalcade* in the summer of 1953, Campbell was one of six persons (out of the ninety six) considered important enough to be identified. The others were Monroe, Madison, Marshall, Philip Pendleton, and John Randolph.

V

The conflict of interests evident in the Virginia Convention was merely the expression at the state level of a struggle which centered nationally around the policies of Andrew Jackson and his party. Jacksonian democracy represented the political self-consciousness and emergence of the common man—the frontiersman of the West and the urban industrial worker of the East.

[11] *Alexander Campbell*, by Benjamin Lyon Smith, Bethany Press, 1930, pp. 172 f.
[12] *Op. cit.*, p. 80.

The relation between state and national interests is seen in the fact that Campbell's county of Brooke voted for Jackson both in 1824 and in 1828.

In all his addresses and votes at the Virginia Convention, Campbell consistently supported such Jacksonian policies as a stronger executive directly responsible to the people, general suffrage, the elimination of property qualifications for voting and holding office, rotation in office, and democratization of the judiciary. In other statements during this period, he showed himself in general agreement with Jackson's opposition to the Bank of the United States and his support of general laws of incorporation and moderate tariff policies. Like Jackson, Campbell was strongly anti-Sabbatarian and enthusiastically approved the Sunday mail report of Richard M. Johnson.

In discussing Jacksonian Democracy in his *History of American Political Theories,* Charles E. Merriam notes that "in the Virginia Convention of 1829-30, there was an animated and extended debate in which almost every phase of political opinion was represented." He then goes on to quote Alexander Campbell—without actually naming him—as a spokesman for Jacksonian principles. Referring to his rejoinder to Randolph, Merriam says: "The reply was made that 'there is no other monarch save King Cypher, King Blood, King Sword, or King Purse.' "[13]

Though he followed the Jacksonian line rather consistently during this earlier period, Campbell soon began to oppose certain practices and policies associated with Jacksonian democracy. He criticized the spoils system, referred to the veto (which first came to prominence during Jackson's administration) as a sign of monarchial power, and made critical references to two of the religious leaders prominently associated with Jacksonian democracy: O. B. Brown and Abner Kneeland.[14]

[13]Pp. 190, 192.

[14]See Lunger, *op. cit.,* p. 140.

In 1836 he reflected the characteristic Whig bias against Van Buren as a man of wealth by referring to the "Patrician Church" in Albany where "Mr. Martin Van Buren and Governor Marcy hold pews." This same Whig fiction of Van Buren as a patrician, who later converted the White House into a palace, is reflected in 1838 in some notes in connection with a visit to Washington. Referring to the President's house and the Capitol as rising "in worldly pomp and splendor," he said: "Every thing appears less and less Christian and Republicun" [sic] since "we last visited the Metropolitan City."

In 1840 the Whig candidate for president was William Henry Harrison. During the campaign, Campbell reportedly asked John Rudolph which of the candidates he thought would get the Ohio vote. Rudolph replied: "General Harrison." To which Campbell responded: "I hope it may be so. I will vote for him myself, as he is my personal friend and I approve his policy."

My study of the subject convinces me that Campbell all along was at heart more of a Jeffersonian than a Jacksonian Democrat. Like the sage of Monticello, the sage of Bethany was a thoroughgoing agrarian, with a distrust of the city, an idealization of the gentleman farmer, and a view of society as constituted by independent and relatively equal yeomen. Jeffersonian and Jacksonian versions of democracy differed in their concepts of "the people." For Jefferson "the people," in whose hands political power was to be vested, were in the main, farmers and residents of the villages and small towns. The propertyless city masses had not yet become a factor in the national politics. But in the Jacksonian version of democracy "the people" included, as an important element, the urban workers, many of whom were untutored and without property.

His agrarian and essentially aristocratic point of view led Campbell finally to react against what appeared to be the "excesses" of Jacksonian democracy, and made him ultimately more at home among the Whigs.

VI

Campbell's attitudes toward America and her democratic institutions also show significant shifts.

Upon his arrival in the United States Campbell was an ardent patriot. He gloried in the freedom of his adopted land. In a letter to an uncle in Ireland, he exclaimed:

"I cannot speak too highly of the advantages that the people in this country enjoy in being delivered from a proud and lordly aristocracy . . . I would not exchange the honor and privilege of being an American citizen for the position of your King."[15]

Following the Virginia Convention experience, he not only became more conservative in his political views, but less sanguine regarding American democracy. The reasons are many: Among them are: his taste of power politics in the Virginia Convention, the violation of the rights of the Cherokee Indians by the state of Georgia, the failure of the Virginia Assembly to do anything constructive following the slave revolts of 1831, the mounting evils of slavery, the bitter controversy over abolitionism, and the rising threat of Roman Catholicism.

In 1833, he wrote:

We begin to doubt the permanency of our own political institutions; and men are now proving that no parchments, constitutions, or forms of government can throw efficient barriers in the way of cupidity, ambition, and pride of man.[16]

An abrupt change in his attitudes can be seen during and following his visit to the British Isles and the continent in 1847. By contrast with what he saw there, the American system now shone in all its earlier glory. Writing from England he used language reminiscent of Thomas Paine in describing the evils of the British system, which permitted a few aristocrats to live in

---

[15]Richardson, *op. cit.*, I., 465 f.
[16]*Millennial Harbinger*, 1833, p. 121.

pomp and luxury amid the "squalid poverty and wretchedness" of the poor. He wrote of the evils and the inequity of the law of primogeniture, by which twelve of the sons of a nobleman "must be comparatively poor that one of the thirteen may be exuberantly rich." In the cities, especially London, he reported seeing

> thousands of little children in the streets, bearing all the insignia of squalid, wretched poverty. . . . No school for them—no table—no bed—no book—no teacher. . . . For every *Prince,* and *Lord,* and *Nobleman,* there are likely thousands of these. For every palace there are multitudes without a cottage, a hut, or a home. I ask myself, Is this the price of a splendid monarchy! Are these the conditions on which royal palaces are reared! . . . If so, then let me have a land without palaces, a country without splendid parks and gardens, cities without Gothic temples, a nation without Lords, and a community without beggars, starvation, and pestilence.[17]

After visiting France, he wrote that the United States had risen "one hundred per cent" in his esteem above any country he had seen since he left. He went on to express the hope that the people of his adopted country would "never sell for a mess of pottage their birthrights!!"

Upon his return to America, Campbell, in several addresses, expressed in moving and poetic language his new love for America and her free institutions and his sense of America's God-given mission to the world. For example, in an address before the Philo-Literary Society of Cannonsburg College, Pennsylvania, in 1852, Campbell dealt with "The Destiny of Our Country." There was a note of warmth and devotion in his first reference to "our divinely favored and beloved country." He then drew a poetic and moving picture of the blessings and progress of the American people in the seventy-five years of their existence. He described the beauty of the "thousand hills and vallies, waving in rich harvests, or covered with green pastures, overspread with bleating flocks of sheep or lowing herds

[17] *Ibid.,* p. 574.

of cattle, interspersed with beautiful villas and romantic hamlets." He extolled the courage of the pioneer who opened up the West, "grubbing the virgin earth in quest of his daily bread," and the enterprise of the sons and daughters of the pioneers who had erected "thrones of justice, solemn temples, stately residences, colleges, male and female seminaries [which] every where attest their good taste, their liberality, patriotism, and genuine philanthropy." After speaking more particularly of the progress made in education he concluded by saying that, while patriotism "has no special place in the Christian Religion," it may become a channel by which we can communicate to others blessings which otherwise "no Christian man could bestow upon his species." This is a far cry from the pessimistic, critical attitude which Campbell showed toward the American union in the decade of the 1830's and in the early 1840's.

Campbell's new enthusiasm for American democracy was born partly of love and partly of fear—partly from seeing democracy in a new light against the background of European society, and partly from the fear that, with all its shortcomings, it might be destroyed as a result of the deepening slavery crisis and the threat of Catholic subversion.

VII

Campbell was outspoken in regard to most of the public issues of his time. He opposed woman suffrage, considered Roman Catholicism a threat to American institutions, advocated free public schools, opposed the manufacture and sale of alcoholic beverages, sought the elimination of slavery, defended capital punishment, opposed the Mexican War, and was an ardent pacifist. These issues he dealt with—often at great length—in the pages of the *Millennial Harbinger* as well as on the lecture platform.[18]

---

[18]All of these topics are explored, with considerable documentation, in *Political Ethics of Alexander Campbell*. To most of the topics entire chapters are devoted.

His attitudes on many of these questions were conditioned somewhat by the fact that he was situated geographically almost at the intersection of the frontier and the Mason-Dixon line—the two axes around which some of the chief political issues of his period revolved. As a resident of the Virginia panhandle he reflected frontier interests as against the entrenched financial power of the East—especially during his earlier Jacksonian period.

In the matter of slavery, he was squarely "in the middle." In relation to "the unfortunate controversy between slavery and anti-slavery," he wrote, "we are, perhaps, on the most neutral ground, as a county, that could well be imagined. We are in a slave state, it is true; but almost literally without slaves." This helps account for the fact that Campbell's position on this controversial issue seemed to satisfy extreme partisans of neither the North nor the South.

His views on many of the other subjects with which he dealt also reflect in some degree this geographical location.

VIII

Though he himself was outspoken on the public issues of the time, he opposed what today would go by the name of "Christian social action." He did so fundamentally on two grounds.

One was his insistence upon the separation of Church and State. He opposed the action of religious bodies either in approving or criticizing specific acts of government. This would be to interfere in functions which properly belong to the state. "The Church cannot constitutionally undertake to reform the State," he said in reference to the slavery issue. "It may seek to convert the citizens; but can never assume, by any political expedients, to reform the State."

The other basis for his opposition to Christian political action was his distinction between matters of "faith" and "opinion."

Only those things that are set forth in Scripture "in express terms or by approved precedent" were considered matters of faith and binding upon all Christians. Other inferences and deductions from scriptural premises fall into the category of "opinion" and cannot be made terms of communion. This distinction, taken together with the principle of individual interpretation and carried over into the field of ethics, means that for Campbell a church can take a stand *as a church* on a moral issue only where the Bible's commands are clear and unmistakable. Social ethics, therefore, must remain largely a matter of individual interpretation and judgment.

Another and very practical factor contributed to Campbell's stand against even the *discussion* of highly *controversial* issues in the church. This was his fear that it might divide the church. After noting how the slavery controversy was dividing the Methodist, Presbyterian, and Baptist bodies along the Mason-Dixon line, Campbell once went on to say: "We are the only religious community in the civilized world whose principles (unless we abandon them) can preserve us from such an unfortunate predicament."

I have elsewhere attempted to point out what seemed to me to be some of the graver shortcomings of Campbell's position in this regard.[19] But this must be said in its favor: the church's most important role in regard to social and moral issues is not convention resolutions or local church pronouncements. Rather it is the day-to-day action of individual Christians, like Campbell himself, speaking out on the vital issues of the day and using their influence—both in the arena of public opinion and at the polls—on the side of what they consider to be right.

On this latter point Campbell speaks a pertinent word:

> In our country and government, every man is responsible for his vote. When, therefore, in his horizon, there is a question or a crisis involving, as he judges, any good, or the prevention of any evil,

[19]See Lunger, *op. cit.*, pp. 269-272.

it is his duty to God, who gives him a vote, and it is his duty to man, to use, or to give that vote, to that person, or to that measure, which will, in his judgment, inure to the most good, or of two evils to prevent the greater, by voting for the less.[20]

The problem which Campbell and his generation have left for us to solve is that of developing educational techniques by which individual Christians can be motivated and then give some guidance and support as they seek to fulfill their responsibilities as Christian citizens.

---

[20]*Millennial Harbinger,* 1857, p. 174.

Alexander Campbell and the Judgment of History

EVA JEAN WRATHER

Biographer of Alexander Campbell

I

The life of every man whose chosen work causes him to move in the bright glare of the public domain must bear two judgments: the judgment of his own contemporaries, and the judgment of history.

With some men, these judgments are not hard to come by. In achieving fame, they walk a relatively simple and direct path to sainthood—or to villainy. But with other men, of more complex minds and varied endeavors, the judgments are bound to be more controversial.

One of Campbell's contemporaries, in writing an essay on "Versatility of Talent," sought to describe him: "Alexander Campbell of Bethany, Virginia, is a profound linguist, a revival preacher, a school master, a farmer, postmaster, politician, architect, anatomist, and several other things besides, and cannot be much beaten in any of them by anybody."[1]

It's a fair estimate—if one divorces the adjective "revival" from "revival preacher," and if one places a great deal of emphasis on the "several other things besides," such as: debater and lyceum lecturer; author, editor, and publisher; college founder and college president; and pioneer in the fight for a free public school system.

For, in truth, like Jefferson and Franklin, Campbell was himself a 19th-century embodiment of the renaissance conception of the "whole man"—an ideal fused in his thinking with the Greek ideal of the "middle way," Aristotle's "golden mean," the balanced life of reason, marked by breadth of sympathies, and judgments. He was the true "citizen of the world"—equally at home in a frontier log cabin or a mansion on Tidewater Virginia; equally at ease with an awkard college freshman or a lady-in-waiting at the court of Queen Victoria.

Alexander Campbell and Andrew Jackson were contemporaries, and their fellow citizens were quick to note significant similarities between them.

To begin with, they were much alike in appearance. The Scots-Irish strain showed plainly in both their faces—long, fair, with strongly marked features; keen blue eyes, penetrating but quizzical and humorous, beneath heavy brows; and abundant hair, inclined to be unruly, arching up sharply from high, bold foreheads.

They were much alike in their political philosophies. When Campbell made his one foray into politics to sit, along with

[1]*Periscopes,* by William Elder, 1854, p. 213.

Madison, Monroe, and Marshall, in the distinguished Virginia Constitutional Convention of 1829, he considerably alarmed Eastern conservative delegates at the outset by the jesting assurance that he had come to Richmond with "a pruning knife to lop . . . a few aristocratical branches" off the "venerable" tree of liberty.

At the same time, his deep kinship of spirit with the democratic West did not blind him to the dangers of unbridled democracy in either church or state, nor deter him from satirizing the crudeness either of frontier manners and amusements or of frontier camp-meeting revivalism which he felt outranged religion's intellectual concerns and content. While, like Jackson, he had set his face against every form of government that tends to "make the rich, richer, and the poor, poorer," he would never flatter the ignorant or sentimentalize the improvident.

By canny and thrifty business management, he built a small inheritance of some three hundred acres and a modest house into a manorial estate of over fifteen hundred acres and a "mansion" of some twenty-five rooms. He imported French wallpaper for the walls of his guest parlor, in the same design chosen by Jackson for the graceful hallway of his Hermitage; and the Campbell household was reared in strict regard for "good manners" as one of the "seven fine arts." Indeed, Campbell's Bethany and Jackson's Hermitage alike gave the lie to those Eastern aristocrats who liked to assume that all life West of the Alleghanies was wild and uncouth.

Both he and Jackson were actuated by a high Puritan conviction of the sacredness of stewardship, To those who would criticize his wealth as unworthy a Christian reformer, Campbell once bluntly replied: "Be assured, gentlemen, that we desire to be still richer" in order "to have it in our power" to propagate still more vigorously the principles of Reformation; and, certainly, had the master of Bethany not made the fullest use of his talents, there would have been no printing press and no college there to spread abroad this message for almost half a century.

Finally, Campbell and Jackson were very alike in temperament. Both men strode through life with the free and determined tread of a Highland chieftain. Both men were born to be passionately loved—and passionately hated.

James Madison, who often heard Campbell preach in Richmond while they were sitting together in the Constitutional Convention, declared: "I regard him as the ablest and most original expounder of the Scriptures I have ever heard." Robert E. Lee, after reading his "Address on Colleges," compared him with Milton as a man who, if he had been delegated as a representative of his species to one of the many Superior worlds, would have suggested a grand idea of the *human race*." Henry Clay introduced him to embassies abroad as one of "the most eminent citizens of the United States." Andrew Johnson extravagantly pronounced him, "the greatest . . . reformer since the day of Paul." James A Garfield, his devoted follower, reverently adored him as this "living wonder."

With Campbell, any temptation to arrogance or self-love lurking in such praise was soundly discouraged by his being the recipient of a constant and equally eloquent flow of abuse—and by his own saving sense of humor. As he himself once whimsically put it: "If I am flattered a little now and then, I am sure to find censure as will ballast my cargo beyond the danger of upsetting."

Alexander Campbell had his full share of the pride and self-assurance of the strong man, who inspires in others the confidence he himself feels. But there was about him none of the petty ego and shallow vanity of the small man. Since, as an editor, he always took great pride in printing both sides of any issue, he regularly, and with evident sardonic amusement, published examples of the bitterest invective against himself—from the crude, satiric humor of such widely distributed doggeral verses as "Alexander the Great, or the Learned Camel"; to the solemn anathemas of those who denounced him as a "child of the devil," spreading abroad a "delusive and soul-destroying heresy."

Others classified Campbell and his adherents in biblical terms as those to turn "the world upside down." And on this point—of the revolutionary quality of the "Campbellite" Reformation—friend and foe were alike agreed.

Yet this man whose name was the symbol of such ferment on the American religious scene for half a century—through whose practical leadership and zeal as a reformer there was to develop the one major Protestant movement wholly indigenous to America—this man was not American born or reared.

II

Alexander Campbell was born in the County of Anrrim in North Ireland in 1788—the same year Lord Byron was born—a year at the dawning of the Age of Romanticism—a revolutionary era, with the American Revolution just recently won and the French Revolution about to begin, when peoples on both sides of the Atlantic were throwing off old classic restraints and rejoicing in the birth of new freedoms in literature and art and in political and social thinking.

Young Alex had a good heritage—half Scots and half French—with the two strains mingling richly to form his character. Through his father, Thomas, a Campbell of Clan Argyle, he was heir to the proud fiery, poetic temper of the Scottish Highlander and also to a deep, quite vein of Celtic mysticism. Through his French mother, he was imbued with a spirit of rationalism and a penchant for logic and order; and through her, too, he was heir to all the bold independence of the French Huguenot and to those peculiarly French gifts for ironic wit and joy in the art of living which could fill a country parsonage with love and laughter despite political revolutions and the rigors of plain living enjoined on the family of a dissenting Presbyterian parson in a country where all emoluments and favors went to the privileged clergy of the powerful state church of the king.

As soon as the boy began to manifest that love and habit of scholarship which was to remain with him throughout his life, Thomas Campbell introduced his son to the writings of John Locke; and Alexander was started on his most exciting intellectual adventure. For there—in Locke's concepts of religious toleration and liberty, which had, indeed, marked a watershed in human thought,—the young seeker found his challenge. And there—in Locke's empirical psychology, positing an open world of experiment and observation and reason against a closed world of dogma—the young thinker began to find his method.

Meanwhile, Thomas Campbell had come to know that Ireland, torn by her ancient, bitter religious conflicts, held no peace for him; and in 1807, he hopefully set sail for the New World. The following year, when his family set out to join him, a shipwreck off the Scots Hebrides providentially delayed them and gave Alexander a winter in Scotland, to follow in his father's footsteps to the University of Glasgow.

The experience proved quite as stimulating in the religious as in the intellectual realm, as he explored the great metropolis boasting churches of every persuasion from High Church to Low, from ancient St. Mungo's Cathedral to the newest Haldanian Tabernacle. By the close of his university year the stirrings of revolt against the harsher dogmas of Calvinism, which he had begun to feel long since at home in Ireland, had come full cycle. He formally broke his last ties with the Seceder Presbyterianism of his youth.

He was by no means sure where his new quest might lead him. He only knew that he must find some system of religious truth acceptable to his own independent, critical, inquisitive mind.

Alexander passed his 21st birthday aboard the sailing vessel to America; and as soon as the family was reunited in the frontier village of Washington, Pennsylvania, father and son made a remarkable discovery: in the two years of separation they had traveled much the same spiritual journey.

Eagerly, Thomas put the first proof sheets of a document, which he called a *Declaration and Address*, into the hands of his son; and eagerly Alexander read them. Well he might, for the gentle, irenic Thomas Campbell had written a revolutionary document—an actual American Religious Declaration of Independence. And quite consciously so.

Just as Thomas Jefferson had challenged the American colonies to cast aside Old World political tyrannies by appeal to the "natural" and "inalienable" rights of man, so Thomas Campbell was challenging the citizens of the new Republic to cast aside their bondage to outworn religious creeds and decrees of Old World ecclesiastical councils by appeal to the "fundamental truths" and "first principles" of the New Testament. Making a radical new approach to the old problems of Christian unity and liberty—partly inspired by fruitful suggestion in the American Constitution—he proposed a unity without uniformity in a Christian democracy, where men of many theological opinions would be held together in common acceptance of the one saving fact of the Christian faith, a loyalty to the person of the Christ.

By the time he had read the last page of this long document, Alexander Campbell knew that he had found the answer to his spiritual quest. And, diligently, he returned to his books to put on the armor of knowledge necessary for such a ministry of reformation.

His first year in America was scarcely past until he was ready to step out into a bold role of leadership in the new movement. When the regular Presbyterian Synod of Pittsburgh refused admission to the Campbell reform group, bringing serious charges of heresy against its members, Thomas was disposed to let the matter lie. But not Alexander. He formally answered the Synod and, with sure dramatic instinct, chose a striking and unforgettable figure of speech to impress their thesis of reformation.

The Christ of history, he said, as revealed in the New Testament, had been sent of God to open wide "the gates of Zion" to all who would believe on him. Then, with the passing centuries, there had evolved these elaborations of dogmas and decrees which had gradually "narrowed the gates" until, he plainly asserted, not even the apostle Paul could be admitted according to the creedal standards imposed by the modern sects. But now, Alexander triumphantly concluded, a new reformation was come with the avowed purpose of once more lifting up the New Testament as the only "standard" in order "to open the gates of admission into the Church as wide as the gates of heaven."

Satisfying as such a ringing declaration of faith and purpose might be, a young man of 22 was not giving all his thought to the theological. In the spring of 1811 Alexander married Margaret Brown, and they made their first home on her father's farm in the fertile Buffalo valley of the Virginia Panhandle—the place that was to become Campbell's own "Bethany," his beloved rural "Patmos" which the most flattering offers of great city pulpits, to come in future years, could never tempt him to leave.

In 1812 their first child was born. And this happy domestic event precipitated a theological crisis which sent Alexander to his books for another period of intensive study, this time on the question of infant baptism and its relation to the entire question of the very nature of the Christian faith.

Actually, he had foreordained the issue of his thinking long since in County Armagh. For there, before he was fourteen years old he later recorded, his "infant soul [had] revolted" against the terrible dogma of infant damnation; and, two or three years later, he had rejected a second "item of Calvinistic faith," the doctrine of conversion which bade him believe that depraved man, born to the taint of original sin, can of himself do nothing to work his own salvation but must wait on some miraculous outpouring of the unpredictable, arbitrary grace of God to reveal whether he is of the elect or the damned. Now other powerful forces were at work in Campbell's mind: the Lockian philosophy's denial of the old concept of "inherited guilt" which had provided the rationale for the practice of infant baptism; and an emphasis on new concepts of man's freedom and responsibility which decreed that each man must bear his own judgment for his own sins and that man has an active, not a passive, role in his own conversion.

So, slowly, Campbell came to a whole new conviction: that a great source of both the unity and the power of the "Ancient Gospel" lay in a doctrine of conversion which, through uniting the process of repentance, baptism, and assurance of forgiveness of sins, powerfully embraced the whole nature of man—his reason, will, and emotion—and so restored his active participation in this drama of man's regeneration through Christ's death, burial and resurrection; and that this was a divine mystery most richly and fitly symbolized—as the example of Jesus himself seemed to indicate—in the rite of baptism by immersion. Such a conviction obviously involved so radical a change of view from centuries of Christian tradition and practice that Campbell was convinced it had come to him, not alone by process of reason, but also through some mystical insight, wonderfully lifting him up, as he later wrote, to "a new peak of the mountain of God, from which the whole landscape of Christianity presented itself to my mind in a new attitude and position."

But whatever mystic vision might be involved, there was a practical question that could not be escaped: would acceptance of "believer's baptism" again narrow those gates to Christian communion which the reformers were proposing to open?

Ultimately, Campbell did not think it would be so—provided, as he later admonished, that the sacramental was understood properly as an avenue to spiritual enrichment of the church on earth and not as "the door into heaven." Indeed, from the beginning, the Reformers had adopted the practice of the weekly communion of the Lord's Supper, conceiving it the original center of love and unity in apostolic worship. Now Alexander was gradually evolving a complex view which perceived of faith as "*the principle*" and the Holy Ordinances as "the *means* of enjoyment" of the grace of God; and this was a view, he believed, combining essential emphases of both the High Church and the Low Church elements in Christian thinking whose challenge must be met in any ecumenical councils in the future.[2]

These attitudes would be many years in developing. In the summer of 1812 Alexander Campbell only knew that he himself must be baptized in accord with this new conviction. After some anxious soul-searching, Thomas followed his son's example. In a short time, so did most of the members of the little Campbell reform group; and by this action they reopened a door to communion with a major Protestant body, as a Baptist Association invited their group to membership. Moreover, the action also tacitly acknowledged that leadership of the reform movement had now, in fact, passed from the elder to the younger Campbell—an eventuality doubtless evident to the discerning since the occasion, almost two years earlier, when it was Alexander, and not his father, who had stepped forward to champion the principles of the *Declaration and Address* against the heresy charges of the Synod of Pittsburgh.

---

[2]*Millennial Harbinger,* 1834, p. 423; *The Christian System,* p. 174. See "Catholic Elements Among the Disciples," by Charles Clayton Morrison, in *The Christian-Evangelist,* January, 1938; *What Churches of Christ Stand For,* by William Robinson, 1926 pp. 57 f.

Already it was thus plain that while Thomas Campbell's was the quiet, inner strength of a Melanchthon, his son's was the bold, aggressive strength of a Luther. Nonetheless, a Baptist historian later quite accurately observed that, until the year 1820, Alexander Campbell had not made "much noise in the world."

The occasion to alter the situation came unsolicited, at first almost unheeded—when Campbell accepted a challenge to debate only after some months of hesitation, due largely to his father's strong disavowal of "verbal controversy." But America was just entering an era when the debating platform—along with the various city and town athenaeums, lyceums, and Mechanics' Institutes—was to assume a major role in the "higher life" of adult citizens as a means of both instruction and entertainment; and, more alert to the social environment than his father, Alexander perceived that, especially in the West, the measure of a man was likely to be taken by his ability to maintain his position—religious or political against every thrust of wit or argument of a skillful opponent in debate.

In Campbell's own first experience something else was quite evident; he defended the Baptist side of the argument in very Campbellian fashion, and the interest of his audience was unmistakable—so much so that he ventured to publish the discussion, and the book rapidly ran through two editions.

Alexander Campbell, age 34, had discovered his medium: the power of the press to disseminate the principles of reformation.

In characteristic bold action, he sent across the mountains for the best press and compositor he could find to set up his own printing office near a convenient ford in the Buffaloe; issued a prospectus for a monthly magazine; and, as became an editor announcing himself as a champion of American Religious Independence, dated his Preface to the first number July 4, 1823. It was a little magazine, unprepossessing in appearance and in title—*The Christian Baptist* was its name. But within a few months it was making the name "Campbellism" a by-word in the West. There was constructive theological discussion in the magazine, and passages of eloquent appeal for Christian unity and toleration. But these things were not the hallmark of *The Christian Baptist.*

For fourteen years, Thomas Campbell's *Declaration and Address* had been before the public; and its irenic, gently persuasive voice had largely fallen on deaf ears, unheeded. To the author's son, it seemed plain that the reason must lie in the "spiritual lethargy" of the churches themselves—complacent in their divisions, refusing to sweep from their minds what John Locke had called the "rubbish of the ages" and to rethink their past daringly and creatively so that the church might worthily meet the challenge of a new age of freedom and enlightenment.

Therefore, with his *Christian Baptist,* Alexander Campbell set out deliberately to make the voice of reform the voice of thunder. He would be another prophet to call the churches to repentance, another Athenian gadfly to sting the people awake from their apathy. Though knowing full well that prophets are generally stoned and gadflies given the hemlock to drink, he would mercilessly seek out every weakness and error of traditional theology, every failure and hypocrisy of the historical church. To his task he brought a gift for striking paradox, satiric exaggeration, and ironic wit whose French accent was quickly recognized by those who soon dubbed him "the Voltaire of the Mississippi Valley." But to may other citizens of this Western land, the editor of *The Christian Baptist* spoke with the authentic voice of their America—a voice worthy of those who took pride in calling themselves "men of the Western Waters" because they felt as free as those waters to seek their own destiny, religious or political.

Viewed in its larger context, Campbellism was a new and virile phase of that revolt against Calvinism which the philosophy of the Enlightenment had long since inspired in independent minds of both Old and New England to whom the old dogmas of the original sin, total depravity, and predestination no longer seemed valid mirrors of man and society. Campbell's was the age of Channing, Emerson, Parker, and the flowering of New England Transcendentalism, where Utopias flourished and very man, as one wit said, carried "a scheme for reform in his vest pocket." Though Alexander Campbell usually thought of himself as a man of the 18th century—guided by reason, suspicious of "enthusiasm," averse to all fanaticisms—he was in many respects a child of his own romantic era. Indeed, what more utopian than his and his father Thomas' own dream of a "purified, united household of God"? And for the next three decades, not even the lectures and essays of Emerson would exhibit a more exuberant democratic faith than those of the younger Campbell. In relation to the revolt against Calvinism, Campbell in the West and the intellectuals of New England were engaged in much the same war.

There were, however, significant differences. Always, the East tended to face toward the Old World, and Transcendental Unitarianism was clearly marked by its debt to an alien German metaphysics. But Campbellism spoke in the clear, familiar accents of Locke and Jefferson and Jackson. It was a liberal faith, but it was also a robust faith without vagueness or evasion, possessing a positive content that Western men could understand. Campbell would always retain a strong vein of Calvinistic realism; and those citizens of the frontier, tempered in the struggle against an untamed wilderness and hostile Indians, would admire a religious editor who could challenge them to Utopia and yet keep his feet on the ground; who could combine a spirit of optimistic self-reliance with a wholesome respect for the harsher realities of man's nature and existance.

Then, in 1829, Robert Owen, already famous on two continents as a skeptic and radical socialist, challenged the clergy of America to debate. Alexander Campbell accepted and for eight days they met in Cincinnati in a discussion publicized throughout America and Great Britain.

Some eight years later, in another historic eight-day debate at Cincinnati—with the Roman Catholic Bishop, John Purcell—Campbell was to stand forth as the Prostestant champion of religious liberty. But the Owen debate covered a far broader scope—as attested by a felicitous letter Campbell received from his native land, informing him: "All parties in Ireland rejoice . . . that the *Emerald Isle* produced a Sampson to combat the great Goliath of Deism and Atheism."

Moreover, it was a battle that the editor of *The Christian Baptist* was particularly fitted to wage, for he and Owen started from many of the same premises. Both were idealists and reformers, deeply concerned about social, economic, and political justice. Both were children of the age of the Industrial Revolution which, while opening a new world to man's ken, had also opened new avenues for man's exploitation of man, as Owen and Campbell alike had seen blackly evident in the teeming factory slums of Glasgow. Both were disillusioned by the failure of the church to meet the challenge of the new conditions, and by the ugliness of religious warfare and ecclesiastical pretensions to authority over the minds and consciences of men.

With Owen, this disillusionment had led to bitter conviction that religion itself was "the real source" of mankind's "vice, disunion, and misery." With Campbell, the disillusionment had led to a distinction more perceptive: something was indeed wrong with the church of history, but not with the truth of religious experience; and if, through the years, many unwilling agnostics found their doubts resolved in the philosophy of Campbellism, it was because they saw in Campbell himself a man who could search out the historic sins of the church as honestly and fearlessly as any Voltaire or Tom Paine or Robert Owen, and who could labor to open the gates of the church to the forces of new light, new truth—and yet not surrender the stronghold of his Christian faith.

The Owen debate was far more than another Christian apology in answer to skepticism. Less than twenty years later—and at a time when Campbell himself was traveling abroad on the continent—two young German radicals, Karl Marx and Friedrich Engels, were busily operating from Paris and Brussels to formulate the revolutionary doctrine which by the end of 1847 they would publish to the world as the *Communist Manifesto.* Robert Owen was their true progenitor—young Engels, in fact, having earlier been active in the Owenite movement in England—and Alexander Campbell brought the most mature gifts of his learning, logic, wit, and eloquence to exhibit the fallacies and absurdities of this new religion of a mechanistic and communistic "social system." With his own philosophy deeply rooted in the individualism and independence of an agrarian democracy, he would be unmoved by the mass psychology being generated by the rising industrialism of his age; and as a Christian statesman he believed that, ultimately, the regeneration of society can be achieved only by regeneration within the hearts of men, never by imposing from without any scheme of materialistic humanism such as Robert Owen set forth on the debating platform at Cincinnati.

By the end of this dramatic year of 1829—distinguished by the Owen debate in the spring and the Virginia Constitutional Convention in the fall—it appeared plain that Alexander Campbell, age 41, was at last making considerable "noise in the world."

But it was not a "noise" to please the dedicated Calvinistic Baptists with whom the Reformers had been in uneasy communion for some fifteen years. And so—even as Luther and Calvin and Wesley and other reformers before him—Campbell was to be denied the role of a leavening, transforming influence within the existing body of the church and, instead, was to be forced out into leadership of a new body.

To signify the change, in 1830 Alexander Campbell ceased publication of *The Christian Baptist* and begun publication of a new magazine.

He could lay aside the old without regret. After seven years before the public, its voice of thunder had clearly been heard in the land. "Light is certainly increasing," he reported, " . . . the mountains of discord diminishing, and the deep vallies which separated christians, are filling up." Therefore, announcing himself ready to lay aside his role as iconoclast—"An audience has been obtained, and consequently," he wrote, "the means to obtain it are no longer necessary." The editor optimistically called his new magazine *The Millennial Harbinger* in full confidence that it would, indeed prove a "harbinger of better times"; and, for the next thirty years, he made it his herald of constructive reform.

As a sober realist, he advocated a distinctive name for the new movement—the *"Disciples of Christ"*—and occasionally acknowledged this separateness by speaking of the Disciples as a "denomination." But he never allowed "*the* Reformation of the Nineteenth Century" to forget its high origin and unique mission in the cause of Christian unity; and he considered it a happy augury when the "Disciples" formed a union with an earlier reform movement in Kentucky, the "Christians" under the leadership of Barton Stone. At the same time, throughout the years, he urged Disciples to every co-operative endeavor with other denominations, from Sunday School Unions to a great "Evangelical Alliance" in 1846. For, observing with wry humor that "half a loaf is better than no loaf at all" and that it behooves "Protestant parties [to] come together" in an attitude of "mutual sympathy" to look at each other's warts and wens," he was willing to recognize that such endeavors at co-operation and federation were necessary in order to prepare the way for any true "Catholic" and organic unity to come.

Both Thomas Campbell and Barton Stone were contemplative theorists and men of almost naïvely nontheological casts of mind that made them more adept at proposing a general and generous plan of Christian unity than at executing the plan through a long-sustained campaign of theological discussion and debate. Alexander Campbell's was a virile, critical temper and theologically sophistocated cast of mind to realize that even the noblest concepts of unity and freedom must be tested in the fires of constructive debate and that the structure and content of the ecumenical church itself must be patiently hammered out on the hard anvil of free discussion. When the Reformers were separated from their established communions, his was the capacity for sustained creative endeavor that molded the new Movement into a coherent, major voice in American Christianity.

It was no swift or easy achievement. Even while Campbellism, as one disgruntled observer remarked, became "a raging epidemic" and a *British Millennial Harbinger* began publication in order to carry this "voice from America" into religious consciences abroad, Campbell unhappily observed that the remarkable growth of the movement was bringing its own penalties through an influx of "untaught converts" and "unsent, unaccomplished, uneducated, advocates"; and finally feeling "the spirit of the Christian Baptist" once more "groaning within" him, he unsheathed his sword of attack in the hope of reforming this group of Reformers.

Ironically, the chief trouble obviously lay in a perversion of one of the cardinal principles of the Reformation itself, enunciated by him as "A Restoration of the Ancient Order of Things." Seeming not to perceive the imperative to unity that illuminated this original declaration, some Reformers, Campbell bluntly charged, were forging new bonds of legalism by rummaging "the apostolic writings with the . . . expectations of a

Jew in perusing the writings of Moses" and were themselves displaying an "unhallowed partyism" by their indiscriminate and often illiterate assaults on the whole fabric of every other sect and system in Christendom.

To crown the irony, and being a man possessed of the capacity to look at himself with a certain amused self-detachment, the editor of *The Millennial Harbinger* could not fail to see that some of these distortions of the restoration movement might all too clearly be laid at the door of the editor of *The Christian Baptist;* and, after twenty years' experience, he ruefully admitted that he had both written and spoken some things "which ought not have seen the light."

Actually, part of the difficulty lay in those pressures of leadership which would always force Campbell to write as he ran. Frequently he arose at four in the morning and prepared enough copy before breakfast to keep his presses busy through the day, so that it was little wonder if his language was sometimes more provocative than judicious and his literary style often turgid and verbose because he did not have time to be lucid and concise; and, after a quarter of a century as aneditor, he was plaintively to record, "While I would rather be an author from choice, I am an editor from necessity." The polished volumes bringing together the consistent body of his thought, which he longed to write, were never to be written; and those who would gain access to his mind were left to do so through the media of more than fifty volumes of miscellaneous writings.

If Alexander Campbell was not always understood as he wished, there was a still more cogent reason. It lay in the complex, far-ranging, catholic quality of his mind—always demanding the search for the "rational mean" and the "whole" view of man and issues; probing now one facet of a problem, now another, sharply questioning all simplifications-by-formula, whether the religious absolutes of creed and confession or the secular absolutes of an Owenite social system—a quality which would forever make him the despair and vexation of those who would demand direct and simple judgments and conform religion and society to neat blueprints.

A volume of essays which all literate America was reading in the 1840's was to voice the era's most famous rejoinder to such small conforming minds, everywhere, in a stinging, penetrating passage that read:

> A foolish consistency is the hobgoblin of little minds, adored by little statemen and philosophers and divines. . . . Speak what you think now in hard words and to-morrow speak what to-morrow thinks in hard words again, though it contradict everything you said to-day. . . . Socrates [was minsunderstood], and Jesus, and Luther . . . . . and Newton. . . . . To be great is to be misunderstood."[3]

Even as Emerson was publishing these words from Concord, Campbell was giving his own answer from Bethany in an equally pertinent passage where he warned his readers that, in the never-ending quest for truth, man must constantly seek "correction and enlargement" of his views and always "act under the conviction that we may be wiser today than yesterday."

Alexander Campbell would never seek solutions in words alone; and from his action in this crisis of the reformation, there was to flower the richest and most congenial achievement of his life.

Man's freedom, he believed, is founded upon religion, upon the spiritual conception of man's "rank and dignity" in the universe; and, in turn, he said: "Religion is founded upon learning." "Colleges and churches go hand in hand in the progress of Christian civilization."[4] And so, in 1840, he founded his college at Bethany—and, characteristically, set the date for its annual commencement exercises on July 4.

---

[3]"Self-Reliance," in *Essays,* by Ralph Waldo Emerson.

[4]*Millennial Harbinger,* 1846, p. 408; 1854, p. 61; 1838, pp. 529f.

There, for the next quarter century, he sought to educate young gentlemen of the new republic in the best traditions of renaissance learning and discipline. Indeed, he liked to emphasize that the Revival of Learning had been the direct "harbinger, or cause, of the Protestant Reformation" itself. And young men at Bethany, under President Campbell, would be constantly reminded of their rich heritage in this alliance between scholarship and Reformation; they would find Luther and Bacon, religion and the new science, dwelling comfortably together in their classrooms.

The college bell awakened the students every morning at dawn, and the day began with the assembling of the entire student body for the President's lecture on sacred history. It was a unique course of lectures, illumined by the gifts of an exceptional teacher; and he himself was proud to point out that it made Bethany the first college in the country to teach the Bible in nonsectarian fashion as that great library of sacred history and literature which is the common treasure and foundation of Western culture.

However pleasant the prospects at Bethany, Campbell sadly confessed that his later decades knew "no more golden years."

The black tragedy of the ever-mounting sectional bitterness between North and South lengthened its shadows even over Bethany. Repeatedly, during the years of controversy, Campbell used all the eloquence of his voice and pen to warn the nation against the threat of its fanatical extremists—those "one idea good men," whom he considered the most dangerous of all men, because their irresponsible oversimplification of complex, troubled issues makes impossible that whole and rational appraisal which alone can resolve such issues with peace and justice. When the final rupture came, he could take satisfaction in the knowledge that his own pleas for the "middle way" of tolerance and understanding had so prevailed that Disciples of Christ did not permit their political differences, North and South, to break their Christian bonds.

He could not stay from his own household the personal tragedy of a war between brothers. His eldest son was a colonel in the Confederate army—his favorite nephew editor of the first Republic newspaper in Virginia, the most persuasive influence on Lincoln's decision to recognize the new state of West Virginia. The cousins did not speak again until they met at the bier of Alexander Campbell in 1866.

III

The reformer, born to revolution in North Ireland, died to another revolution called Reconstruction in America. Yet busy city editors laid aside their preoccupations with the dilemmas of President Johnson and the Freedman's Bureau to note the passing of "this remarkable man." One editor summed up the judgment of many when he wrote: "Theologians in the old world, as in the new, revised their opinions and overhauled their dogmas by the light of his giant mind."

Even at the hour of his death, dissident voices were still to be heard, hopefully relaying the prediction that there were no shoulders to receive "his mantle" and so, with Campbell's passing, his whole movement would soon "explode or crumble." Disciples would prove the prediction false as they continued, however hesitantly and falteringly at times, to carry forward the movement dedicated to their historic goal of seeking to open wide the gates of Christian communion and co-operation.

Yet, Alexander Campbell personally was to experience a strange fate. In the 1890's, less than thirty years after his death, a young Disciple minister in New York, distressed to observe that several recent works on religious reformers had dealt with lesser men while omitting the name of Campbell altogether, sharply charged his churchmen: "Lest some few should call us 'Campbellites' we would suffer the name of a great man to die."

The charge fell, unanswered, into a great void. A generation later, Disciple pulpits were more likely to call on the authority of Luther or Calvin than of Alexander Campbell, and general works of American historical scholarship appeared unaware of his place or influence. History seemed about to record its most damning judgment—the verdict of silence.

Today, however, there is evident in many directions a virtual renaissance of interest in Campbell, the man and the theologian. One evidence, of course, is this series of lectures, being sponsored at Bethany College. Another is in a stream of new books on Campbell; and still another is in the new Disciples of Christ Historical Society building at Nashville which, through the media of both art and literature, is impressively featuring his contribution to American religious thought.

Many reasons might be assigned for this curious course that the judgment of history has taken in respect to Alexander Campbell.

The most obvious of these reasons lies, ironically, in the nature of Campbellism itself. For Campbell deliberately engrained his adherents in the nonhistorical approach of Lockian philosophy and constantly urged upon them the dictum, "call no man master upon the earth." Disciples of Christ imbibed this philosophy of independence so thoroughly that the most terrible of all epithets to their ears became that of "Campbellite," and they have virtually made a cult of denying their "Campbellism."

In the 1890's a young New York minister may have protested this attitude in vain. But, today, Disciples of Christ have grown into a new maturity of historical perspective. They are beginning to acknowledge that the strength of any people is rooted in its past; and on the indelible record of their own past, they must admit that it is Alexander Campbell's name which is written the largest.

This era of his neglect may also have been due in part to a more subtle influence.

As the Disciples moved out of their own zealous early period of pioneering reform and themselves tended to settle into a certain comfortable respectability and even conformity, they increasingly found Alexander Campbell a disturbing man with whom to live. By contrast, Thomas Campbell and Barton Stone were easy and comfortable heroes for the church. The editor of *The Christian Baptist* had admittedly come not to bring peace of mind but to arouse the church to that searching self-examination which is the hallmark of the mature mind. He constantly holds up the mirror in which Disciples—even as the rest of Christendom—must behold their own imperfections.

Therefore, many Disciples—perhaps in unconscious justification for seeking to escape this probing gaze—have appeared strangely prone to take their own estimate of Alexander Campbell's religious character and contribution from the mouths of his detractors and, like his contemporary misinterpreters, to refuse to see him whole and so damn him by half-truths. Stranger, still, even some Disciples who would admit that the contribution of a Luther and a Melanchthon or an Abelard and a St. Francis, are not to be measured by the same rule, have nonetheless been prone to castigate Alexander Campbell because he was not of the temper of a Thomas Campbell or a Barton Stone.

Today, there is heartening evidence that the church everywhere is awakening to a need to search its own soul anew and, as always in a sober and imperiled world, is ready again to listen to its prophets, even to heed the sting of its gadflies. Disciples of Christ are sharing in this mature mood of self-examination; and one of its first fruits is a renewed appreciation of the sharply prophetic voice of Alexander Campbell.

Another, and perhaps major, reason for this changing cycle of neglect and appreciation of Campbell lies, of course, in the very fact of this changing cycle of time itself.

In the deceptively secure and naïvely optimistic world of the early 1900's young men, convinced that scientific humanism held the answer to all problems of human society and all questions of human destiny, could easily pronounce outdated the philosophical theology of Alexander Campbell, with its stern definition of the historical process in terms of its relation to the sovereignty of God and man's need for the community of redemption. When new discoveries in biblical criticism and archeology outmoded some of Campbell's presuppositions, young men —reacting all the more strongly because of the overeffulgent praise of their fathers—deemed it a sign of their emancipation to deprecate the whole fabric of Campbell's Christian system.

In the chastened, stricken world of the 1950's, amid the ruins of its fallen idol of man's arrogant self-sufficiency, Alexander Campbell speaks out with sometimes startling relevance.

He was, of course, a man of the 19th century with his knowledge necessarily limited by the intellectual boundaries of that century; and he made no claim to infallibility of vision concerning the problems of a redeemed and united church. If he did not have—or claim to have—all the right answers, he did raise most of the pertinent questions and point in many of the directions which the theology of the 20th century is finding most fruitful to explore.

Wherever study conferences of the ecumenical church may gather, provocative contribution to their discussions is to be found in Campbell's thinking on such central issues as the relation of reason and revelation, of liberty and authority; in his perception of a simple confession of the Lordship of the Christ as the only basis and only hope of unity between Christians; in his unique conception of an "ethical sacramentalism" enshrining belief in dramatic symbol and channeling the senses of the whole man—body, mind, and spirit—into enjoyment of the grace of God. Indeed, it is in this full-length view of the "whole man" that Campbell's thought seems especially pregnant today, positing a philosophy of true Christian humanism which encompasses both man's possibilities and his limitations and reconciles man's freedom with God's sovereignty.

Perhaps, above all, the very temper of Campbell's mind is perennially relevant to the problems of a divided church. For through his dedication to the constant quest for new light, new learning, and through his intellectual honesty and humility bidding him always remember that he might be wiser today than yesterday, he helped produce that climate of inquiry which alone can resolve difficulties in the free and creative exchange of question and opinion and idea.

If history is at last beginning to write its judgment on Alexander Campbell, it undoubtedly will not reflect the judgment of an extravagant contemporary who predicted that Campbell will "yet shine as the brightest star in the galaxy of all reformers," forming "the central figure in the historic group of Savonarola, Huss, Wyclif, Luther, Calvin, Knox, Zwingli, and Wesley."

History will almost certainly accord him a high seat at the ecumenical council tables of the world—there, in his clear and virile and peculiarly American voice, to speak out the eternal challenge of Christian liberty and the Christian hope.